Praise for *Napoleon*

W9-CCM-063

"[A] succinct yet lively biography . . . [A] very readable and entertaining biography." —*The Washington Post*

"Paul Johnson . . . is a historian at the top of his game. His judgments are sure. His historical range is sweeping. His storytelling is crisp and his writing elegant."
—*The Oregonian*

"[Paul] Johnson is a brilliant writer, fluent, precise, crisp, and in full command of the music of words."
—Michael Pakenham, *The Baltimore Sun*

"The selection of the venerable British historian . . . Paul Johnson to write on Napoleon . . . has turned out to be a wise one: Johnson is succinct, critical, and deeply skeptical of the Napoleonic legend."
—*The Atlantic Monthly*

"Lucidly written, and enlivened by personal details and well-chosen quotations. It offers the bones of that remarkable career and some attempt to situate its wider significance within the sweep of modern history." —*TLS*

"Johnson's sharp-edged view of Napoleon is well supported, and well worth considering." —*Kirkus Reviews*

"This splendid addition to the Penguin Lives series offers a comprehensive view of Napoleon in all his incarnations. . . . Fascinating and instructive." —*National Review*

"Johnson provides an excellent overview . . . [He] presents a concise appraisal of Napoleon's career and a precise understanding of his enigmatic character." —*Booklist*

PENGUIN BOOKS

NAPOLEON

Paul Johnson is an acclaimed historian whose many bestselling books—including *Modern Times*, *A History of the American People*, and *The History of Christianity*—have been translated into numerous languages. A frequent contributor to publications such as *The New York Times*, *The Wall Street Journal*, and *The Spectator*, he lives in London.

PAUL JOHNSON

NAPOLEON

A Life

A LIPPER™/PENGUIN BOOK

PENGUIN BOOKS

Published by the Penguin Group

Penguin Group (USA) Inc., 375 Hudson Street, New York, New York 10014, U.S.A.
Penguin Group (Canada), 90 Eglinton Avenue East, Suite 700, Toronto,
Ontario, Canada M4P 2Y3 (a division of Pearson Penguin Canada Inc.)
Penguin Books Ltd, 80 Strand, London WC2R 0RL, England
Penguin Ireland, 25 St Stephen's Green, Dublin 2, Ireland (a division of Penguin Books Ltd)
Penguin Group (Australia), 250 Camberwell Road, Camberwell,
Victoria 3124, Australia (a division of Pearson Australia Group Pty Ltd)
Penguin Books India Pvt Ltd, 11 Community Centre, Panchsheel Park, New Delhi - 110 017, India
Penguin Group (NZ), 67 Apollo Drive, Rosedale, North Shore 0632, New Zealand
(a division of Pearson New Zealand Ltd)
Penguin Books (South Africa) (Pty) Ltd, 24 Sturdee Avenue,
Rosebank, Johannesburg 2196, South Africa

Penguin Books Ltd, Registered Offices: 80 Strand, London WC2R 0RL, England

First published in the United States of America by Viking Penguin,
a member of Penguin Putnam Inc. 2002
Published in Penguin Books 2006

5   7   9   10   8   6   4

Copyright © Paul Johnson, 2002
All rights reserved

THE LIBRARY OF CONGRESS HAS CATALOGED THE HARDCOVER EDITION AS FOLLOWS:
Johnson, Paul, 1928–
Napoleon / Paul Johnson.
p.   cm.—(A Penguin life)
"A Lipper/Viking book."
Includes bibliographical references.
ISBN 0-670-03078-3 (hc.)
ISBN 978-0-14-303745-3
1. Napoleon I, Emperor of the French, 1769–1821.   2. France—History—1789–1815.
3. Emperors—France—Biography.   I. Title.   II. Penguin lives series.
DC203.J5   2001
944.05'092—dc21
[B] 2001045605

Printed in the United States of America
Set in Bulmer
Designed by Francesca Belanger

Contents

Contents

FEW INDIVIDUALS have had more impact on history than Napoleon Bonaparte. He is the grandest possible refutation of those determinists who hold that events are governed by forces, classes, economics, and geography rather than by the powerful wills of men and women. Though Bonaparte exercised power only for a decade and a half, his impact on the future lasted until nearly the end of the twentieth century, almost two hundred years after his death. Indeed, his influence may not yet be spent. People love reading about him and his spectacular rise, just as in Roman and medieval times they read about Alexander. And they ponder the question: Might I, in comparable circumstances, have done as well? Few persons of ambition have failed to see Bonaparte as an exemplar or a spur. It is significant how many of those who exercise various forms of power, and wish for more—media tycoons, for example—have decked their offices or even their persons with Napoleonic memorabilia.

It is one of the contentions of this book that Bonaparte was not an ideologue but an opportunist who seized on the accident of the French Revolution to propel himself into supreme power. I say "accident" because the example of Britain and the Scandinavian countries showed that all the desirable reforms that the French radicals brought about by force and blood could have been achieved by peaceful means. As it was, the horrific course of the Revolution led, as was almost inevitable, to absolutism, of which Bonaparte was the beneficiary. And once installed in power he relentlessly sought further power by extending his rule to encompass most of Europe. It does not seem to have occurred to him to study the example of his older contemporary George Washington, who translated military victory into civil progress and renounced the rule of force in favor of the rule of law. But Bonaparte always put his trust in bayonets and cannon. In the end, force was the only language he understood, and in the end it pronounced a hostile judgment on him.

In the meantime, though, Bonaparte unleashed on Europe the most destructive wars the continent had ever experienced. For the first time, large-scale conscription played a notable part in swelling the armies, and their encounters became battles of entire nations. As the wars proceeded, the military casualties increased relentlessly, but the civilian populations also suffered in growing measure. First Italy, then Central Europe, finally Spain and Russia became victims of Bonaparte's wars of conquest. The German-speaking lands in particular were fought over again and again, and the eventual revulsion against Bonaparte played a critical part in creating a spirit of German nationalism that was to become aggressive and threatening itself. A new concept of total warfare was born, and alongside it grew other institutions: the secret police, large-scale professional espionage, government propaganda machines, and the faking of supposedly democratic movements, elections, and plebiscites. France herself, though fought over only in the final phases of the wars, suffered bitterly, and some of her losses were permanent. At a time when other European populations were growing fast, France's slowed down and began to stagnate, and in due course France inevitably began to slip from her position as the leading power in Europe to second-class status—that was Bonaparte's true legacy to the country he adopted.

The statesmen who gathered in Vienna after the military collapse of Bonapartist France were determined to restore not only the old legitimist thrones but, so far as they could, the old conventions and rules of law that had kept the peace, or limited the impact of hostilities when war broke out. The Congress of Vienna must be regarded as one of the most successful peace settlements in history. With some exceptions, it determined the frontiers of Europe for a century, and though it did not prevent all European wars, it made a general conflagration far less likely. The nineteenth century was, in general, a time of peace, progress, and prosperity in Europe, until the old system finally broke down in 1914–18.

Thereafter, however, the Bonapartist legacy, aided by France's decision to treat the dead ruler as a national hero and exemplar to the world, came into its own. The First World War itself was total warfare of the type Bonaparte's methods adumbrated, and in the political anarchy that emerged from it, a new brand of ideological dictator took Bonaparte's methods of government as a model, first in Russia, then in Italy, and finally in Germany, with many smaller countries following suit. The totalitarian state of the twentieth century was the ultimate progeny of the Napoleonic reality and myth. It is right, therefore, that we should study Bonaparte's spectacular career unromantically, skeptically, and searchingly. At the beginning of the twenty-first century, anxious as we are to avoid the tragic mistakes of the twentieth, we must learn from Bonaparte's life what to fear and what to avoid.

NAPOLEON

CHAPTER ONE

The Corsican Background

NAPOLEON BONAPARTE was born on 15 August 1769 at Ajaccio on the island of Corsica. It is a paradox that this man who thought in terms of conquering entire continents should have had his life bounded by three islands: Corsica, less than half the size of Wales, no bigger than Vermont; Elba, much smaller, where a parody of his glory was enacted; and Saint Helena, a mere speck on the ocean, his death-prison. It was a vintage time to be born: 1769 was also the birth year of Bonaparte's nemesis, the duke of Wellington, and the politician who backed him, Viscount Castlereagh; and in and around this date were born many of the greatest spirits of the coming age: Chateaubriand and Madame de Staël, two more of Bonaparte's dedicated enemies; Wordsworth and Coleridge, who cursed him in prose and verse; Beethoven, who dedicated his *Eroica* Symphony to the First Consul, then tore out the page in anger when he became emperor; and a host of others—Hegel and Schlegel, Andrew Jackson and John Quincy Adams, George Canning, Metternich, and Sir Walter Scott.

It was a vintage year in other ways. The Industrial Revolution was just taking off in Britain, with textiles leading the way; and Captain Cook, landing at Botany Bay, brought the final continent, Australasia, into the West's compass. But

Corsica was very remote from these and other great events. It was poor, wild, neglected, exploited, politically and economically insignificant. Exactly a hundred years later, the English artist Edward Lear descended on the island with his sketching materials and produced a scintillating visual record of its appearance, unchanged in a century: spiny, vertiginous mountains, almost impenetrable pine forests, vast fields of rocks and rare cataracts, and endless barren scrubland, known locally as *le maquis,* a word that was to become synonymous with guerrilla country. Its total income was tiny. The courts of Europe regarded it as almost worthless. The British took it twice in the eighteenth century, and twice relinquished it as more trouble than it was worth. It had belonged for hundreds of years to the Italian city-state of Genoa, which had acquired it in the age when Genoa was, next to Venice, the richest maritime power in the Mediterranean. But Genoese rule had never penetrated much inland from the sea towns, Bastia, Calvi, Bonifaccio, and Ajaccio. There was no profit in it. So local insurgents ruled the interior and occasionally struck at the walled coastal towns. In the 1760s, increasingly weak Genoa turned to the French for assistance, which the French provided. But they disagreed with Genoa's policy of allowing in the hated Jesuits, banned in France. They withdrew their forces, and in 1767 the insurgents took Ajaccio. For Genoa, this was the last straw, and in 1768 it sold the entire island to France by treaty, in return for a paltry sum. This was a critical event for Bonaparte for, born the next year, he automatically became a French citizen.

Not everyone despised Corsica. In his *Du contrat social*

(1762), Jean-Jacques Rousseau remarked that, while government corruption was universal in Europe, one tiny country was still capable of legislating against it, in a spirit of primitive simplicity. That was Corsica, and he added that he had a presentiment that this island of nature would one day astonish Europe. In consequence, the sage was invited by the insurgents to come to Corsica and draw up a constitution, which would serve when they won their independence by the sword. He did not go. But he persuaded his young friend James Boswell, the future biographer of Dr. Samuel Johnson, to include the island in his grand tour, and arranged for him to see the leader of the insurgents, Pasquale Paoli, who bore the title of "General of the People." Boswell went, formed a lifelong admiration and friendship for Paoli, and left a vivid record of his journey, both in his diaries and in the book about Corsica he published on his return to Britain. The book made him famous—he was known as "Corsica Boswell"—and it was widely read in Europe. Among his readers was the young Bonaparte. It gave him ideas.

Not that Bonaparte ever had the ambition to become Corsica's liberator. That was Paoli's thankless role, and a small-time part at best. To people of Bonaparte's background, the future lay not inland but outward—on the high seas and the great landmasses beyond. People moved into and out of Corsica all the time. Among the ambitious of the coastal towns, there was no such thing as the timeless stability of the interior. The Bonapartes originally came from the minor nobility of sixteenth-century Tuscany. In Ajaccio they had become, as it were, hereditary lawyers, while retaining their titles of nobility, sixteen quarterings (ancestors with titles of nobility), and so forth. They operated on a small scale and were just rich enough to own their own house and garden and to employ servants. Carlo Mario da Buonaparte, as he called himself, married the fourteen-year-old Letizia, also of distant Italian noble extraction, but from a family that had heavily intermarried with the squireens of the wild interior. She gave him eight children who lived, of whom Napoleon, or Nabulion as he was registered, was the second. The name, eventually to give itself to an age, was of no significance. The father, from some notion of family *pietà,* simply repeated the name given by his great-grandfather to his second son. Bonaparte scarcely ever used it. An analysis of Napoleonic autographs, of which thousands exist, shows that he always signed himself Buonaparte, then later Bonaparte. This was the name by which all his friends, and even his first wife, Josephine, knew him and addressed him, both officially and familiarly, and it is the name I use throughout this book. When he became emperor, he reluctantly adopted Napoleon as his name, for reasons of royal protocol, and his second wife called him such. But he rarely signed the name Napoleon in full, simply scribbling "Nap" or "Np"; and sometimes he forgot his new rank and signed "Bonaparte."

Bonaparte has had more books written about him than any other individual, with the sole exception of Jesus Christ. They continue to appear at brief intervals, especially in English and French but also in many other languages, and they are read: publishers regard a Napoleon book as more likely to sell, by virtue of its subject alone, than any other biography. Nearly all these books speculate on the family or genetic origins of Bonaparte's soaring ambitions. Virtually all agree that the hardness in his nature came from his mother, not his father, an apparently ineffectual person who died young. Madame Mère was of sterner stuff. Some biographers therefore see his bellicosity as deriving from his wild Corsican forebears, with their cult of the iron law of revenge, the vendetta. Oddly enough, the one form of ferocity in which Bonaparte was a little deficient was revenge; he was uncharacteristically, if unpredictably, forgiving of injuries—not always or even usually, but often enough to surprise. Beyond reading Boswell's book and deriving from it lessons that had nothing to do with the island, he took no interest in the place once he had left it. He never visited it. It never figured in his geopolitical calculations. On the other hand, he gave no sign that he was ashamed of his origins. He simply dismissed it from the forefront of his mind as carrying no importance in the economy of his ambition.

The alternative theory of biographers is that Bonaparte was a throwback to the distant *condottiero* of his Tuscan ancestors, a soldier of fortune who would sell his sword to whoever would pay handsomely for it, and found a dynasty on the profits of war. It is true that, until France took over in 1768, Corsica looked to Italy, which was much nearer, and supplied its written language and culture. But Bonaparte never showed any affection for Italy as a country—he agreed with Metternich's definition of it: "a mere geographical expression"—and when he called his son and heir king of Rome, he was reincarnating a quite different and much earlier entity. He showed no sentiment toward any of its historic cities either, treating them like mere gold or silver coins to be snatched from enemies and awarded to members of his family or allies. The Italians themselves he despised.

Looking outward, to the sea, as a Corsican in Ajaccio would, he formed a boyhood admiration for the Royal Navy, which rode the Mediterranean waters, so far from home, so confidently. He expressed a desire to join the British navy as a midshipman cadet, and in due course to command one of those wonderfully polished, burnished, pipe-clayed, and smartly painted—and formidable—three-deckers that occasionally anchored in the harbor. But that required money, and even more "interest" (influence or pull), neither of which his family possessed. So the moment passed. But it is curious to reflect on this, his earliest ambition, and to wonder at how differently history would have evolved had his boyhood whim been satisfied. As a boy Bonaparte was distinguished by his gift for mathematics, which remained with him throughout his life and was of inestimable value in his profession. But it would have served him well at sea, too, and there can be no doubt he would have risen high in naval service and become a rival to Nelson. As it was, the sea, so inviting to ambitious Corsicans, became and remained his mortal enemy. He did not understand its true strategic significance, and the naval dimension of geopolitics always eluded him—his last, terminal mistake was to step aboard the HMS *Bellerophon*, on 15 July 1815, never to be a free man again. Bonaparte's bitterness against the British sprang partly from his belief that the power their supremacy at sea gave them was somehow unnatural, even unfair. It was his frustration at the unjust success of blockade that led him into the endless labyrinth of the Continental System, which proved a salient part of his undoing.

The only other occasion when Bonaparte offered his sword as a mercenary was when, already trained and commissioned as an officer in the French army, but angry at slow promotion, he considered serving the sultan of Turkey, as many European officers did at that time. But an opportunity to serve France in higher rank came just in time, so this moment passed, too. Bonaparte was not by temperament a mercenary. But he was not a patriot, either. He was not moved by sentiment, secular or religious. If metaphysical forces played on him at all, he was a victim of superstition, though a willing one. He believed in his stars, like the ancient Romans he admired (insofar as he admired anyone). He felt he had a destiny, and most of his life he was confident in it. But, sure as he was of what destiny intended for him, he nonetheless was determined to wrest it from events with his own brain, arms, and will. In his material calculations, he was quite clear and consistent. He needed not a paymaster, like a mercenary, not a disembodied ideal, like a patriot, but a source of power, so that he could capture it and obtain more power. So he asked himself: Where does the nearest source of real power lie? And the answer came immediately: France.

Hence the significance of Bonaparte's birthdate, which made him a subject of the French crown. And there was a further stroke of fortune. From 1772 to 1786, the virtual ruler of Corsica, or rather of the walled coastal cities, was a Breton nobleman, the comte de Marbeuf. He built up his own local party, which included Carlo Bonaparte. Carlo was almost penniless but he had his sixteen quarterings, so Marbeuf was able to send him to Versailles as a representative of the local nobility. He was away some time, and while so, Marbeuf, aged sixty but a lifelong womanizer, had a leisurely affair with Letizia (or so the evidence suggests). In return, he made use of a fund that, every year, awarded 600 places at high-class French schools to the children of poor French parents who could prove their *noblesse*. The family could do that, if nothing else, and on 31 December 1778, young Bonaparte, aged nine, was gazetted by the ministry of war with a place at a royal military school. His elder brother, Joseph, was similarly privileged, and Marbeuf arranged free places for both of them at a preparatory school at Autun.

Hence, at the end of the following year, Bonaparte and brother Joseph left for France, to learn French in the first instance, from there to be enveloped in the public service of the Bourbon monarchy. A year at Autun was followed by five years at the military college at Brienne and a year at the academy for officers in Paris. These seven years marked the transformation of Bonaparte into a professional French soldier. He was struck by two things. The first was the comparative luxury in which mere cadets lived, being privileged beneficiaries of the ancien régime. He cut all this out when he acquired a say in how the French army was run—all its components, officers included, had to acquire their comforts by their ability to win and their rapacity in securing the trophies of victory. Second, he realized how important it was to make use of his capacity for figures. This got him through the academy (forty-second out of fifty-eight) and a commission as a second lieutenant in the La Fère regiment of artillery, a good starting point for a subaltern without the money or influence needed to serve in smart guards or cavalry outfits. But, more important, Bonaparte began to pay constant attention to the role of calculation in war: distances to be covered; speed and route of march; quantities of supplies and animals, and the vehicles required for their transport; rates at which ammunition was used in varying engagements; replacement rates of men and animals; wastage figures from disease, battle, and desertion—all the elements of eighteenth-century military logistics. He made a habit of working these things out in his head, so that they could easily be dictated for orders. He also became a master map reader, with a gift amounting almost to genius for visualizing terrain from a two-dimensional, often fallible piece of engraved paper. Few young officers of his day had this skill, or bothered to acquire it. Asked how long it would take to get a siege train from the French fortress of Verdun to the outskirts of Vienna, most officers of the day would shrug bewildered shoulders or make a wild guess. Bonaparte would consult a map and give the answer in exact days and hours. This calculating approach to war made Bonaparte more than a tactician. He had the makings of a strategist—indeed, a geostrategist.

In the meantime he matured fast, reaching his full height of five feet five, pale, thin, saturnine, with lank dark hair over a broad brow. Not interested in food or drink, he ate his meals, if he had any choice in the matter, in ten minutes and never caroused. No one ever saw him drunk. He was not exactly a loner, because he liked to lay down the law to comrades. But he could be solitary and he made no lifelong friends at the college or the academy. Boyhood, even youth, fled swiftly. In February 1785, his father died of stomach cancer. Though still only fifteen and the second son, Bonaparte took over, by general consent, his father's place as head of the family, in preference to the amiable but unassertive Joseph. A year older, Joseph (1768–1844) had decided to forgo a military career and to become a lawyer like his father. He was to be a willing but ineffectual tool in Bonaparte's rise and fall. The next brother, Lucien (1775–1846), was more amenable to Bonaparte's schemes, serving him as a soldier and later as king of Holland; but ill-health and lack of enthusiasm forced him to abdicate in 1810, when he faded from public life. The youngest brother, Jérôme (1784–1860), who most resembled Bonaparte in his vigor and enthusiasm, was rewarded with the kingdom of Westphalia and served in many of the great campaigns, including Russia and Waterloo, after which he went into exile until Louis's son, later Napoleon III, restored the family fortunes in France. Of Bonaparte's sisters, the eldest, Eliza (1777–1820), married a Corsican, Prince Bacciochi, whom Bonaparte made prince of Piombino; but she left him soon after and was made grand duchess of Tuscany. Pauline (1781–1825) was the most beautiful of the girls and married in turn Bonaparte's West Indian commander, Charles Leclerc, then the Roman prince, Camillo Borghese, in whose family palace Antonio Canova's reclining, seminude statue of Pauline can still be seen. The youngest sister, Caroline (1782–1839), the most untrustworthy, married Bonaparte's cavalry commander, Joachim Murat, and in due course the couple were made king and queen of Naples. It has to be said that Bonaparte did the best, according to his lights, for his siblings, provided they obeyed him. He showered on them and their spouses principalities and kingdoms, but all were lost, and all his siblings met misfortune or underwent long years in exile.

But at the time the sixteen-year-old Bonaparte took over direction of the family fortunes, all this was in the future and all were young. His father left virtually nothing. The youth's pay was ninety-three livres a month, of which room and board took twenty. It was little more when he was promoted first lieutenant in 1791. His problem was to ensure that his mother's widowhood was honorable and that his brothers and sisters did not starve. In the artillery *parc* at Valence, he tried to educate himself by intensive reading, as the young Winston Churchill was to do during his Indian service. He still wrote letters in Italian, though his French, grotesquely misspelled, was improving. He read Plato's *Republic;* Buffon's *Histoire naturelle;* Rousseau and Voltaire; James Macpherson's Ossian works, those bibles of the early Romantics; various histories and biographies; and a volume, in English, of English history, which he read with particular attention, believing England to be a successful country, well worth studying for its secrets—though he never seems to have grasped the essence of the English constitution, then regarded as its chief virtue. He took copious notes, chiefly of statistics. But he read fiction, too, historical romances chiefly. He also wrote fiction, including a short story set in London in 1683, about Whig plotting against Charles II, in which macabre murders, reformist politics, and divine retribution are strangely mingled.

He also began, but never finished, a history of Corsica. He could not finish it because he kept changing his mind about what Corsica's future should be. Before he died, Carlo Bonaparte broke with General Paoli and the cause of independence. Paoli never forgave the family, whom he classed as traitors and foreigners. In 1789, the new French National Assembly allowed Paoli, who had been in English exile, to return to Corsica. He at once set about organizing an independent republic there. Between September 1786 and June 1793, Bonaparte returned to Corsica four times: first as a moderate supporter of French power, in gratitude to Marbeuf; then as an open critic of an increasingly oppressive French regime, run from Paris; then as an outright supporter of Paoli and a colonel in the Corsican militia; finally as a critic and opponent of Paoli, who not only showed him no favor but exercised dictatorial powers and proposed to separate Corsica finally from France. At this point Bonaparte threw in his lot with the Corsican Jacobins. Civil war broke out on the island in April 1793. For Paoli, who had become increasingly suspicious of the young, swiftly rising soldier, with his French training and education, this was the end. He had the entire Bonaparte family publicly sentenced to "perpetual execration and infamy." Thus indicted in a land where the vendetta ruled, all of them, the mother included, ran for safety to France, never to return.

Though it is clear Bonaparte had bitter memories of his native isle, and wished to erase it from his mind, it did provide him with something important: a map of the kind of power he sought. Though Paoli became his enemy, he remained in a sense Bonaparte's hero-mentor. For Paoli was not a warlord, or at any rate not just a warlord, as all his predecessors in the struggle for independence had been. He was a man of the Enlightenment who believed—as did Jefferson, Adams, and Washington on the far side of the Atlantic; Burke and Fox in England; and Lafayette in France—that revolution and armed struggle were no more than the necessary prelude to creating a humanitarian republic endowed with an ideal constitution. He was the man Rousseau had been looking for to turn little Corsica into a model commonwealth, an example to all Europe for the wisdom of its laws. Paoli emerges from Boswell's copious writing and much other evidence as noble, disinterested, fearless, and sensible; a man who had absorbed in exile British pragmatism and, like the Founding Fathers in America, blended it skillfully with the more abstract idealism of Rousseau, Diderot, and the *encyclopédistes*. He seized with both hands the opportunity to treat Corsica, as Rousseau had envisaged, as a tabula rasa on which could be inscribed a scheme of government and code of laws that would make it, though small and weak, a world exemplar. Alas, his sword was not strong enough to win and maintain Corsican independence alone, and his British ally deserted him, so that he, too, ended his life in exile.

But the archetype of Paoli, not just conquering soldier but supreme legislator and enlightened ruler as well, became part of the furniture of Bonaparte's mind. He was already seeking power, but the fate of Corsica enabled him to give a purpose to power. Winning a battle, a campaign, a war, was not an end in itself but an opportunity to impose a new order on the old corrupt and inefficient systems. He was to be a Paoli for all Europe, built in an incomparably larger mold and operating on a continental, perhaps a world scale, for the better governance of mankind. He did not realize, and perhaps he never realized, that there was a fundamental contradiction in this vision. Whereas Paoli, acting on behalf of the Corsicans themselves, was a mere liberator who then legislated with their consent, Bonaparte, with his overarching scheme for Europe, was not so much a liberator as a conqueror, and the violence of the conquest was incompatible with the idealism planned for the subsequent government, which thus became mere occupation by force, unjust and cruel. Warfare, from being a means to an end, became an end in itself, and Bonaparte, having once unsheathed his sword, found it impossible to lay it down for long. He ended by being no nearer his goal, and no safer, than his last victory—thus inviting inevitable nemesis. All this seems clear enough to us now. But nothing was clear then, in the early 1790s, except that the world could be reorganized afresh—that all Europe was a tabula rasa—and that a bold soldier was exactly the man to write his destiny on it.

CHAPTER TWO

Revolutionary, General, Consul, Emperor

REVOLUTIONARY FRANCE of the 1790s provided the perfect background for an ambitious, politically conscious, and energetic soldier such as Bonaparte to make his way to the top. It demonstrated the classic parabola of revolution: a constitutional beginning; reformist moderation quickening into ever-increasing extremism; a descent into violence; a period of sheer terror, ended by a violent reaction; a time of confusion, cross-currents, and chaos, marked by growing exhaustion and disgust with change; and eventually an overwhelming demand for "a Man on Horseback" to restore order, regularity, and prosperity. Victor Hugo, a child of one of Bonaparte's generals, was later to write: "Nothing is more powerful than an idea whose time has come." It is equally true to say: "No one is more fortunate than a man whose time has come." Bonaparte was thus favored by fortune and the timing of the parabola, and he compounded his luck by the alacrity and decision with which he snatched at opportunities as they arose.

Indeed, if there was one characteristic that epitomized Bonaparte throughout his rise and grandeur, it was opportunism. He was the opportunist incarnate. Few successful men have ever carried a lighter burden of ideology. He had no patriotism as such, for he had no country. Corsica had been barred to him. France was no more than a career structure and a source of power. He had no class feelings, for though legally an aristocrat, he had no land or money or title, and saw the existing system of privilege as a fraud and, more important, as a source of grotesque inefficiency. But he had no hatred for kings or nobles as such. Nor did he believe in democracy or rule by votes.

The people he observed with detachment: properly led, they could do remarkable things. Without sensible leadership, they were a dangerous rabble. He liked the vague and abstract notion of Rousseau's concept the General Will, offering a ruling elite that knew its business the opportunity to harness the people to a national effort without any of the risks of democracy. In practice an elite always formed itself into a pyramid, with one man at its summit. His will expressed the General Will (an antidemocratic notion, in which a nation's will was embodied by one man rather than by head counting) and gave it decisiveness, the basis for action. Constitutions were important in the sense that window dressing was important in a shop. But the will was the product to be sold to the nation and, once sold, imposed. If this be ideology, it was the ideology of an opportunist who could adapt himself to the phases of the revolutionary evolution, as they occurred, until his personal moment came. That was a matter for the stars, and the stars had no ideology, merely motion.

Bonaparte believed not in revolution but in change; perhaps accelerated evolution is the exact term. He wanted things to work better, or more fairly, and also faster. In England he would have been a utilitarian; in the United States, a federalist and a follower of Alexander Hamilton; in Austria, a supporter and goader-on of Joseph II, the archetype of the Enlightened Despot. Europe in the 1780s, spurred on by constitution making in America and by autocratic reform at home, was ripe for change. Virtually everyone wanted it. There was little opposition to it. In Denmark in the 1780s, for instance, prison and law reforms were carried through, poor relief established, land reform introduced, feudal labor services abolished, the slave trade outlawed, outmoded tariffs removed, and commerce liberated, all without the assistance of the mob and without a single riot or political execution. Rather more cautious changes were made in the Netherlands and parts of Germany. If Louis XVI had been more energetic and decisive, France could have followed the same pattern. The aristocracy was crowded with progressive reformers. The royal bureaucracy was keen on improvements. In every ministry, huge dossiers of desirable changes were compiled and plans prepared, most of which were later put through by revolutionaries who claimed credit for them. All that was missing was the decisive impulse from the top. And France, unlike Denmark, was tied to the chariot of its great power status—it referred to itself as "the Great Nation" and sought in the second half of the eighteenth century, almost as a duty, to engage in vastly expensive and increasingly unsuccessful wars to maintain its historical position as Europe's leading country. So the 1780s were a struggle against bankruptcy, leading to financial juggling, arbitrary impositions, court desperation, and finally to the calling of the Estates General in 1789, for the first time in nearly two centuries. After that, the process of change spun out of control.

Bonaparte watched the earlier phases of the Revolution as an outsider who longed to be inside the decision-making process. About 100,000 words survive of his notes on the books he read. He described Cromwell thus: "Courageous, clever, deceitful, dissimulating, his early principles of lofty republicanism yielded to the devouring flames of his ambition; and, having tasted the sweets of power, he aspired to the pleasure of reigning alone." At Auxonne, in April 1789, Bonaparte got his first taste of putting down the mob, commanding small bodies of soldiery that restrained Revolutionary excess at the point of a bayonet, exactly as Cromwell would have done. He translated his Corsican Jacobinism into mainland French terms. The Bastille fell; the Estates General became the Constituent Assembly; Louis was stripped of his executive powers and made a virtual prisoner, and his attempted escape abroad in the midsummer of 1791 ended in disaster. Army officers were asked to take an oath of allegiance to the Assembly in consequence, and most of them, being royalists, refused. Bonaparte took it on 4 July. His view was that Louis should have been banished, not imprisoned and executed, and that the young Louis XVII should have been proclaimed regent. In practice, however, he threw in his lot with the republicans. It became increasingly clear to him that the Bourbon monarchy was finished, the king a doomed puppet. On 20 April 1792, the moderate Girondin ministry forced Louis to declare war on Austria, and on 15 May on Sardinia. The

Revolutionary slogan soon became: "War with all kings and peace with all peoples." Bonaparte, who was rarely less than a realist, knew this was rhetorical nonsense, but he could accommodate it. No professional soldier ever regards the declaration of war as an unmitigated evil, and the prospect of general war in Europe was enticing. War meant promotion, bigger commands. On 30 August 1792, Bonaparte was promoted to captain, backdated, with arrears of pay. Civilian Europe entered a dark age, but good times for the warriors had begun.

In February–March 1793, Revolutionary France declared war on Britain, Holland, and Spain. Civil war broke out in Brittany and the Vendée. In the south the royalists tried to take Marseilles and succeeded in seizing the great naval port of Toulon. On 29 August they were joined by British and Spanish units, under the protective shadow of the Royal Navy. Bonaparte had called attention to himself by writing and publishing a call for national unity, a pamphlet entitled *Le Souper de Beaucaire;* he had also been engaged, in Valence, in reequipping and retraining the artillery. In an inspired moment, the war commissioners in Paris sent him to Toulon. He arrived there on 16 September and at once reorganized the artillery of the besieging forces. Within weeks his decisiveness, professionalism, and ingenuity made him effectively the director of operations, though he was much junior in rank and age to the nominal commanders. There were some brilliant future generals in this operation, too: Marmont, Suchet, Junot, Desaix, Victor, and others. But it was Bonaparte who planned the assault and led it on 16 December. General Du Teil recommended him to Paris thus: "I lack words to list Bonaparte's merits: much science, and equal intelligence, and perhaps even too much courage." He added: "You, the Ministers, must consecrate him to the glory of the Republic." The recklessness with which the young man exposed himself while storming Toulon was remarked, indeed, by both sides. The great English historian G. M. Trevelyan recalled: "I once came across the following item of intelligence while turning over the files of an English newspaper of 1793: 'Lieutenant Buonaparte has been killed in one of the recent encounters before Toulon.'" He added: "Everything I have learned since has increased my regret that the news proved inaccurate." Bonaparte not only survived but was immediately promoted to brigadier, skipping the ranks of major and colonel.

Toulon, then, launched Bonaparte's career. He was now known. But it also increased his exposure to danger. The Revolution was devouring its children, even the great Georges Danton, whose motto, *"L'audace, encore l'audace, toujours l'audace!,"* might have been Bonaparte's own. During the Terror, he remained in France, reorganizing the artillery in preparation for an invasion of Italy. It was Augustin de Robespierre, younger brother of Maximilien, leader of the Terror, who was responsible, as army commissioner, for pushing Bonaparte forward, commending his "transcendent merit." But Maximilien Robespierre fell from power on 27 July 1794 and was promptly guillotined. In Nice, where Bonaparte was stationed, he was immediately identified as a Robespierre protégé and arrested. He was right to thank his stars for his survival, for many were executed on much less evidence. But France was sickening of the slaughter, and in September he was quietly released.

Suspicion remained, however, and he was not restored to his prospective command of the artillery for the Italian campaign. But his services were used. Bonaparte now knew as much about cannon, in theory at least, as any officer in the army (many experts had been cashiered as royalists or shot, or were in exile or serving with foreign armies). The artillery textbooks by the comte de Guibert and Pierre-Joseph de Bourcet, which Bonaparte had read, insisted that the whole point of successful use of artillery was to concentrate maximum firepower on one point of the enemy's line, usually the weakest. It was reiterated in a book by Bonaparte's mentor, Du Teil, *L'usage de l'artillerie nouvelle,* which applied the principle to the more powerful and mobile guns now coming into service. This was the work of the comte de Gribeauval, who had been in charge of gun manufacture under the ancien régime. He introduced standardization of cannon design. As a result, the artillery the republic inherited was equipped with standard four-, eight-, and twelve-pounder field guns, as well as a six-inch howitzer (heavier pieces were designated siege artillery). These weapons were considerably lighter than their predecessors, thus increasing their mobility and the speed with which they could be brought into action and resited.

Bonaparte's contribution, therefore, was to accept the basic equipment (though he later replaced the four-pounders with six-pounders and increased the proportion of twelve-pounders), but to ensure that the increased mobility and firepower of the army was used with effect, by rigorous training and practice. Under the Gribeauval system, each regiment was standardized with twenty companies, with its own depot and training unit. It was Bonaparte's aim to ensure that all gunnery officers, and where possible NCOs also, understood the mathematical principles of aiming and could read maps. In theory field guns could fire, unsighted, twelve rounds a minute. Bonaparte thought this a waste of ammunition. But he insisted that the minimum three rounds a minute of aimed shots could be improved, and his tactic of power concentration, of course, helped to accelerate the round delivery from each gun. Cannon were not merely Bonaparte's trade; they embodied the power principle that was always at the heart of his thinking. The object of power, in his view, was not only to crush opposition to his will, but more usually to inspire fear, so that power did not need to be used at all. An opposing army must be made to fear you, because once terror began to creep over it, the battle was half won. The best way to inspire terror, he reasoned, was by the noise and havoc of guns. But they must be accurate, for Bonaparte knew that soldiers, like himself, were fatalistic, especially in facing big guns. They believed that if your "number" was not on a shell or roundshot, you had nothing to fear, and rounds falling harmlessly some distance away reinforced their stoicism. This was Bonaparte's battle psychology, and it is impossible to overemphasize the role cannonading played in his success on the field.

When Bonaparte was released, he was still obsessed by the chance to apply his artillery warfare to the Italian front. During the summer turmoil over Robespierre in Paris, the campaign had been halted, and the Austrians had advanced toward the Genoa coast, with the Royal Navy assisting them at sea. The orders from Paris were to remain on the defensive. But that was contrary to all Bonaparte's instincts, and as soon as he was released he set about persuading General Pierre Dumerbion, the army's commander, a cautious, elderly veteran, to mount a preemptive attack on 17 September 1794. It embodied what was to become another Bonaparte principle—separating opponents and attacking them individually—by driving between the armies of Austria and Savoy. On 21 September, following Bonaparte's plans, the Austrians were surprised and badly beaten at Dego on the Savona River, losing forty-two guns. As this was the first field battle for which Bonaparte was responsible, it is worth noting for its surprise, speed of attack, and point of attack from the rear, a favorite tactic of his where possible. Bonaparte's instinct was to reinforce success by pressing the advance speedily into the Italian plain. But Dumerbion overruled him on 24 September, being anxious to end on a high note, and withdrew to a defensive line. Two months later he retired, but not before he had generously attributed the success of the campaign to his young artillery commander.

Effectively out of a posting, Bonaparte went to Paris, following his principle of going direct to where power lay. His object was to get the ear of the politicians as a military adviser, and from that spring to a top command. His first efforts failed, and it was then in the winter of 1794–95 that he thought of going to Turkey. His eventual success came about indirectly. The National Convention intended to introduce a new republican constitution, to be adopted by referendum. But the participants wished to keep their places and salaries, so an accompanying decree insisted that two-thirds of the seats in the proposed new legislative assembly be occupied by members of the old Convention. This was unpopular, and as a safeguard the regime entrusted Vicomte Paul de Barras (1755–1829) with *plein pouvoir* (unlimited authority) to maintain order.

Bonaparte had got to know Barras, an unscrupulous former royalist officer who had thrown in his lot with the Jacobins, at Toulon. He learned from Barras how effective brutal reprisals against royalists could be, and how the advent of Revolutionary "justice" could be made into an opportunity to amass wealth as well as a chance to grab top positions. Barras had changed coats again in 1794, helping to dismantle the Terror and slaughter those who had imposed it. He was the most powerful single member of the Directory, which succeeded the Robespierre junta. He was already rich, and survived all the various changes and chances of the next two decades to die rich under the Restoration. He was also a highly successful *coureur des dames*. One of his mistresses, in the early 1790s, was a youngish and beautiful Creole widow, Marie-Josèphe-Rose Tascher de la Pagerie (1763–1814). Born in the West Indies, she was six years older than Bonaparte and a fellow aristocrat (by birth and quarterings), but poor and dependent for advancement on her own wits and charm. She had both, and at the age of sixteen she married a better-provided aristocrat, Alexandre de Beauharnais, who sided with the Revolution and became one of its leading generals. They had two children, one of whom, Eugène de Beauharnais, became a key figure in Bonaparte's schemes.

But old Beauharnais fared badly at Mainz in 1793, was accused of treason, and was guillotined. His wife, briefly in prison, could easily have met the same fate. Indeed it is important to remember that virtually all the leading French figures during these years were at one time or another under imminent threat of violent death, and had seen friends, family, enemies, or colleagues go to the scaffold, thus creating the stoicism or indifference with which they regarded the spilling of blood. Without a husband, Josephine kept afloat in Paris society, where she shone in a dim and grisly era, by affairs with numerous politicians, ending with the powerful Barras.

By 1794, however, Barras was after younger prey. But he wished to retain Josephine's friendship and therefore devised a plan to unload her onto Bonaparte, whom he regarded as a promising protégé. Volumes can be, and indeed have been—many times!—written about Bonaparte's relationship with Josephine, but many aspects of it remain obscure and therefore debatable. What seems clear is that initially, at least, the ardor was all on Bonaparte's side. Josephine, who had excellent taste, was taken aback by the limitations (as she saw it) of this short, thin, sallow-faced young soldier, praised to the skies by the oleaginous Barras, for reasons she found no difficulty in divining, with a bright future perhaps but with no obvious advantages to offer her in the present. What pressure Barras put on her to accept Bonaparte's courtship we do not know. More likely, it was the urgings of the young man himself, enacted with all the almost desperate determination of which he was capable, that warmed her to him. She was a sophisticated, *désabusé* woman—that I suspect was the chief reason Bonaparte fell for her, a type he had not come across before—but she could be hotly responsive once aroused.

In any case, by the time they were ready to marry, Bonaparte's position had again been transformed. Opposition to the Convention, discredited by its self-perpetuation plan, rose during the summer and early autumn of 1795. Parts of Paris were still almost entirely medieval, with narrow streets fringed by rookeries of crumbling, many-chambered houses, in which thousands of the poor lived and groaned. They could form a vast mob at short notice, capable of overawing troops without decisive commanders. But there were at least three mobs: the Jacobins, the most desperate; the royalists, now scenting a wind of change; and the so-called *modérés*. Elements of all three joined hands in early October to destroy the Convention. Barras did not trust the loyalty of the nominal commander of the Troops of the Interior. He gave the second-in-command place to Bonaparte, and with it effective control of the regular units in Paris.

On 5 October 1795 (13 Vendemière by the new republican dating, soon to be abandoned), about 30,000 malcontents, many armed National Guardsmen, a Revolutionary force now obsolescent, were on the Paris streets. Bonaparte decided to use artillery, the embodiment of his fear principle. That meant choosing his ground carefully and encouraging the mob to move into open spaces, near the Tuileries Palace and the Church of Saint Roche, which they had made their headquarters, where the guns could sweep them with their fire. It also meant a careful choice of shot. Ball or shell was most effective against regular troops. Bonaparte preferred musket balls encased in tins, known as canister or caseshot, or in canvas bags, known as grapeshot. The advantage of grapeshot was that it scattered over a wide area, tending to produce a lot of blood and often maiming its victims, but had to be fired at close range. It rarely killed and thus, while effective as drastic crowd control, did not enable opponents to create the myth of a "massacre." Its aim was to frighten and disperse. Bonaparte took a great risk in maneuvering his guns to point-blank range to give the mob "a whiff of grapeshot," as he put it. It was more than a whiff, of course: a number were killed or died of their wounds. But it ended the attempted coup forthwith, and with it the Revolution itself: the era of the mob yielded to a new era of order under fear. The shotmarks on the façade of Saint Roche are still there to mark the decisive moment. Bonaparte was both the instrument and the beneficiary. Old General de Broglie had advised King Louis XVI to use grapeshot six years before. He had been ignored, and ruin had followed. "Now," as Thomas Carlyle put it in his epic book, "the time is come for it, and the man; and behold, you have it; and the thing we specifically call *French Revolution* is blown into space by it, and becomes a thing that was!"

After Toulon and Dego, Vendemière was Bonaparte's third widely publicized success. All were achieved by cannon. He blew himself into the stratosphere of power from the brazen mouth of his own guns. He was now commander in chief of the interior troops, but he wanted the supreme command in Italy. That, he calculated, would have been Caesar's choice. A general who commands the home front is, ex officio, a man of great political power. But one returning from a campaign of victory and conquest abroad has the nation at his feet, as well as an army behind him. So Italy was what he asked for, and got.

It has often been argued that Bonaparte got the Italian command through his friendship with Barras and his willingness to take Josephine, Barras's discarded mistress, off his hands by marrying her. But it is more likely that he would have got the command anyway, since Lazare Carnot (1753–1823), who had been in charge of France's overall war effort since August 1793, and who strongly approved of Bonaparte's war plan for Italy, felt he was the man to carry it out. Carnot was a Burgundian republican who became a *député* in 1791, and distinguished himself by leading the *levée en masse*, or general uprising, that was the Revolution's reply to the invasion of France by the combined monarchies of Europe. As head of the War Section of the Committee of Public Safety, he reorganized both the army of the Revolution itself, creating thirteen field armies, and the workshops that supplied them with arms, and the methods by which they were financed. He thus produced, as it were, the raw material, in human terms, with which Bonaparte fashioned Europe's largest and most successful war machine. And he did more. He seized upon the semaphore system, invented by Claude Chappe in 1792 and installed between Paris and Lille, to construct a national communications system between the capital and France's frontiers (often beyond), which enabled military messages to be carried at about 150 miles per hour in clear weather. This fit almost magically into Bonaparte's strategy of speeding up the movements of French armies. He also, to Bonaparte's delight, improved the cartographic resources of the army and concentrated its central command into what he called the Bureau Topographique, the first general staff in history.

It was to Carnot that Bonaparte submitted, early in 1796, a revised plan for the invasion of Italy. It was duly approved by the Directory, and Bonaparte was appointed. He left for Italy two days after his wedding. He had already, in effect, ended the Revolution itself. His assumption of the new command marked another historical turning point: the moment when the republican regime moved from the defensive to the large-scale offensive and became an expansionist force, determined to roll up the old map of Europe and transform it on principles formed by its own ideology.

This program could not have been successfully carried out without Bonaparte—that is certain. But equally certain is that Bonaparte would not have possessed the ruthless disregard of human life, of natural and man-made law, of custom and good faith needed to carry it through without the positive example and teaching of the Revolution. The Revolution was a lesson in the power of evil to replace idealism, and Bonaparte was its ideal pupil. Moreover, the Revolution left behind itself a huge engine: administrative and legal machinery to repress the individual such as the monarchs of the ancien régime never dreamed of; a centralized power to organize national resources that no previous state had ever possessed; an absolute concentration of authority, first in a parliament, then in a committee, finally in a single tyrant, that had never been known before; and a universal teaching that such concentration expressed the general will of a united people, as laid down in due constitutional form, approved by referendum. In effect, then, the Revolution created the modern totalitarian state, in all essentials, if on an experimental basis, more than a century before it came to its full and horrible fruition in the twentieth century. It also became, as Professor Herbert Butterfield has put it, "the mother of modern war . . . [heralding] the age when peoples, woefully ignorant of one another, bitterly uncomprehending, lie in uneasy juxtaposition, watching one another's sins with hysteria and indignation. It heralds Armageddon, the giant conflict for justice and right between angered populations, each of which thinks it is the righteous one. So a new kind of warfare is born—the modern counterpart of the old conflicts of religion."

In this awesome transformation, Bonaparte was the Demogorgon, the infernal executive, superbly molded by nature and trained by his own ambitions and experiences to take the fullest advantage of the power the Revolution had created and bequeathed to him. His sensibilities were blunt. His compassion was shallow. His imagination did not trouble him. He had had no religion since (so he said), at the age of nine he heard a preacher insist that his hero, Caesar, was burning in hell. His conscience, never active, was under control. His will possessed his entire being, which otherwise was under no restraints. His capacities were immense. His energy was godlike. Thus, as George Meredith put it, he was "hugest of engines, a much limited man."

Bonaparte's invasion of Italy in 1796, his first strategic campaign as such, was for the French people an imaginative and symbolic success, as well as a military triumph. The

French invasion of Italy at the end of the fifteenth century had ended medieval Europe, and was registered in the French collective mind as a historic event. By resuming the attempt at Italian conquest, Bonaparte struck a responsive chord. It was also, for a Corsican-Italian-turned-Frenchman, the logical thing to do: to conquer his country of ultimate origin and turn it into a dependency of his new *patrie*. But his means were limited. When he joined the army, he found that its paper strength of 43,000 was down to little over 30,000, with only sixty cannon, and that the men were unpaid. His first proclamation (28 March 1796) set the tone of his relationship with his troops: "Soldiers, you are naked, ill-fed. . . . But rich provinces and great towns will soon be in your power, and in them you will find honor, glory, and wealth. Soldiers of Italy! Will you be wanting in courage and steadfastness [to obtain these things]?" From the first, Bonaparte had an implicit contract with his men: they would make his victories possible, and in return he would ensure them loot. More, he would make it easy for their spoils to be transferred back to their families. This made military sense, for it enabled soldiers to save instead of squandering their trophies on drunken debauchery. Needless to say, the officers, especially the divisional commanders, benefited *a fortiori* from this system, and Bonaparte most of all, both on his own account and in the state loot (money in bullion and specie, and works of art) he had transferred to the government in Paris, to reconcile its members to his increasingly high-handed and independent actions. Northern Italy was an ideal field for such a joint-stock looting expedition. Neither the House of Savoy nor the Habsburgs were popular, the small independent states were decrepit, and there were literally thousands of churches, convents, monasteries, and chantries, and valuable paintings and holy vessels in gold and silver, waiting to be pillaged. Bonaparte was careful not to wage war against the church, as earlier republican armies had done, and always stopped his men from slaughtering the clergy, believing them to be a valuable force for social control. But he had no hesitation in "liberating" church property, loading it up on his supply wagons "for safe custody."

Bonaparte had as his chief of staff Louis Berthier (1753–1815), who served him faithfully and efficiently in a variety of senior roles, but mainly as staff chief—he was known as "the Emperor's Wife"—until the abdication of 1814. It was a symbiosis of military minds, as Berthier translated his master's strategic plans into men and matériel and issued clearly written orders to get them into place. Bonaparte owed a lot to him and rewarded him well with lands and titles; he was never quite so effective when Berthier was not there. Bonaparte also had three good divisional commanders, including André Masséna (1758–1817), a former ship's boy, sergeant-major, and smuggler, who became one of the most reliable of subordinates, though with an incorrigible taste for looting (and accepting bribes) that made even his master blush.

Given his limited resources, Bonaparte's invasion of Italy was a daring venture, which repeatedly surprised the Piedmontese and the Austrians with its risky river crossing and speed of attack. He won minor battles at Montenotte, Dego (again), Mondovi, and Codogno; and at Lodi, early in May, he carried off a sensational action in which 3,500 French

grenadiers charged the bridge over the Po and held it against 10,000 of the enemy until Masséna's reinforcements arrived. This delighted the French public, as did the army's triumphant entry into Milan on 13 May, where it was rapturously greeted by the mob, or at least *a* mob, an event made immortal by Stendhal in the opening chapter of *Le Rouge et le noir*. The conquest of Lombardy was essentially a campaign of rivers and bridgeheads. Bonaparte won it against superior Austrian forces, who on the whole fought bravely and stubbornly, by his rapidity of movement, surprise, and tactical ruses. He rounded it up with a famous victory at Arcola, the crossing of the river Alpone, on 15–17 November. This was a characteristic Bonaparte battle. His campaigning style, with its rapid transfers of troops, involved high risks, which sometimes produced potential disasters when faced with a methodical opponent like the Austrians. Bonaparte reckoned to extricate himself from these dangers by his gift of rapid improvisation, his ingenuity, the resourcefulness of Berthier, and the panache of his men. The three-day Battle of Arcola was a classic case of this risky strategy rescued by clever tactics, including a ruse whereby Bonaparte sent a platoon of scouts behind the enemy lines with orders to set up a hullabaloo and persuade the Austrians they were almost encircled. Their hasty withdrawal lost them the battle, and Arcola, like Lodi, became a sensational victory in the newssheets and prints, consolidating Bonaparte's reputation as the republic's most successful general. On 14 January 1797, he won the decisive Battle of Rivoli, leading to the surrender of the last main Austrian fortress at Mantua. In effect the Habsburgs now

withdrew from Italy, leaving Bonaparte to do with it as he pleased.

It was at this point that Bonaparte ceased to be merely a battle general and became also an imperial proconsul, in fact if not yet in name. When he had set out for Italy, his instructions about political arrangements after success on the field had been cramping. They were successively relaxed (or ignored) as he transmitted larger and larger sums of gold and silver to the French treasury in 1796–97. He could thus make his own policies. His technique, adumbrating the Stalinist methods used in Eastern Europe at the end of the Second World War, was to encourage the formation of "patriotic" and republican committees in the main towns, then respond to their requests for independence under "French protection." Thus committees at Bologna and Ferrara repudiated papal rule, and at Reggio and Modena the rule of the local duke. All four, with Bonaparte's encouragement, sent delegates to Milan, and at their meeting declared the formation of the Cispadane Republic, in effect a French puppet state (16 October 1796). The Lombardy towns formed a similar entity called the Transpadane Republic, and Bonaparte knocked the two together to constitute the Cisalpine Republic on 15 July 1797. Meanwhile, he took advantage of a French-organized uprising in Genoa to overthrow the ancient oligarchy there (6 June) and set up what he called the Ligurian Republic. He likewise disposed of the oligarchy in Venice. He supervised the constitutions of the two new states, the first of a score or more he was to create, from his sumptuous viceregal castle at Montebello. He also negotiated the outlines of a peace with

Austria, subsequently endorsed by the Directory at the Treaty of Campo Formio (17 October 1797), under which the Habsburgs recognized the two new French protectorates, surrendered the Austrian Netherlands and the Ionian Islands to France, and (in secret) acquiesced in expanding the French frontier to the Rhine.

This was a huge territorial victory for France and was rightly seen by the French public as Bonaparte's own. Aged twenty-eight, he was now, in military terms, the most powerful man in the republic, a loose cannon, loaded and primed, on the map of Europe, whom the politicians wanted to keep from Paris by giving him fresh assignments well away from the capital—thereby, of course, risking even more spectacular triumphs on his part. Their first idea was to charge him with the invasion and conquest of England. But, having looked at the resources that would be available to him in terms of warships and transports, he would have none of it. It was, he thought, a passport to a watery grave. Instead, he hit upon, and promptly had adopted, a plan that took him a long way from the center of events (which suited the Directors) but was calculated to appeal strongly to the French imagination—the conquest of the Orient.

Interest in Egypt had been growing for a generation, and the first indication of what was to become *le style égyptien* dated back to the 1770s. Bonaparte's objectives, as put to the Directors, were to found a French free-labor sugar-growing colony to replace the West Indian ones; to dig a Suez canal; and to link up with the Marathas and Tipu Sahib, opponents of British rule in India, and help them destroy it. He had vague plans about the vast Turkish empire, too, of which

Egypt was nominally a part. But there was a deeper wish: to play a modern Alexander the Great and acquire rich provinces of inconceivable magnitude. He is said to have remarked: "Europe is too small for me. . . . I must go East." He calculated that with 30,000 French troops, he could raise another 30,000 mercenaries in Egypt, and with 50,000 camels and 150 cannon, he could be on the Indus within four months. He worked all this out down to the last round of ammunition and water canister.

The Directors sanctioned the invasion of Egypt—no more—but laid down that Bonaparte must finance and raise the expedition himself. He took them at their word. He sent his most trusted staff chief, Berthier, to the Vatican to raid its treasury. Guillaume Brune, a notable looter, went to Berne and stole the entire Swiss reserve. Barthélemy-Catherine Joubert forced the Dutch to disgorge. Ten million francs were thus made available, much of it in gold. Bonaparte appointed all the seagoing ships from Genoa and Venice, to add to the Toulon Squadron. The appeal of the expedition enabled him to pick some of the best young officers in the army to accompany him. To sell the project to the French public, he also invited the leading members of the Institut National, created in 1795 to replace the old royal Académie Française and Académie des Inscriptions, to go too. About 160 agreed, and they included some of the best engineers, chemists, mathematicians, historians, archaeologists, mineralogists, geographers, artists and draftsmen, linguists, and writers in France, plus journalists and printers, even a balloonist. It was Bonaparte's first opportunity to engage in large-scale publicity and propaganda, and he made the most of it. Here was not merely a successful general bent on conquest, but the embodiment of French culture, leading a "civilizing mission" to the seat of the world's first urban society.

From first to last, the expedition to Egypt was rich in dramas that provided sensational subject matter for the accomplished artists like Jacques-Louis David and Antoine-Jean Gros whom Bonaparte was beginning to cultivate. By immense good fortune, which Bonaparte continued to enjoy for many years yet, he escaped from Toulon (19 May 1798) without encountering the fleet of the earl of St. Vincent and Lord Nelson, the two British admirals commanding in the Mediterranean. On 12 June, by a combination of threats and bribery, he persuaded the Knights of Malta to surrender their fortress and naval base. He then looted their treasury and ransacked the churches and convents of the island, annexed it to France, and gave it a new government, legal and religious code, and constitution—all in less than a week. Once more evading Nelson, Bonaparte disembarked his men near Alexandria and took it on 2 July. He immediately marched south to Cairo, through the hottest season of the year, dust storms, fly plagues, and appalling water shortages. On 21 July, he drew up his near-mutinous army in squares near the Pyramids, found a field of watermelons that he gave to the soldiers to slake their thirst, issued an Order of the Day to them pointing out that "forty centuries look down upon you," and invited the Mamluk rulers of Egypt to use their ferocious cavalry against his men. They duly obliged, were mowed down by French fire, and got separated from their infantry, which, in due course, was broken by Bonaparte's cavalry. Only 29 Frenchmen were killed, the Egyptians losing more than 10,000, and this easy victory, immediately termed "the Battle of the Pyramids," did wonders for the morale of the entire expedition.

Bonaparte reached Cairo on 24 July. Declaring himself the protector of Islam who had humbled the pope and destroyed the Knights of Malta, he appointed a committee of notables under a French "adviser," designated himself overall ruler of Egypt, nominated a senate of 200 locals, and set about drawing up a constitution. He also founded the Egyptian Institute so his scholars and scientists could get to work.

This scene of peaceful conquest was shattered on 1 August when Nelson destroyed virtually the entire French fleet within the harbor at Alexandria. This left Bonaparte and his army marooned, and it persuaded Turkey to declare war. Bonaparte had other troubles. He received confirmation that Josephine was having an affair, and responded by trying to enjoy the bey's present of an eleven-year-old virgin (unsatisfactory) and a boy (ditto) and forming a liaison with a twenty-one-year-old French girl, Pauline Fourès, his "Cleopatra." He also dealt with a bazaar uprising that killed 250 of his men, exacting the deaths of 2,000 Arabs in consequence, and a fierce outbreak of bubonic plague that killed 3,000 Frenchmen. Despite this, he decided to forestall a Turkish attack by his usual aggressive methods and invaded Syria with 14,000 men, leaving only 4,500 behind in Cairo. He took Gaza, then Jaffa, where, fearing trouble from his 4,500 prisoners, he ordered them all slaughtered, which was done by bayonet thrusting or drowning, to save ammunition. Many women and children suffered in this atrocity, probably the worst of all Bonaparte's war crimes. Plague hit the army again in Jaffa, and Bonaparte—to wipe out the memory of the massacre perhaps, or more likely to provide subject matter for his propagandists—visited the plague hospital to comfort his men. This tender scene was to become, thanks to Gros, the visual climax of the entire expedition.

Bonaparte's small army won some brilliant victories against larger Turkish forces, but he failed to take Acre, stoutly defended by Turks under the command of the English admiral Sidney Smith (whose subsequent windy tales of his exploits won him the nickname "Long Acre"). This was Bonaparte's first major military defeat, and it discomposed him. He decided to return to Egypt with his diminished force of 8,000 men, but ran into a terrifying sandstorm in the Sinai desert. This retreat was an adumbration in miniature, had he only known it, of his future disaster in Russia. At the time, the setback merely confirmed his resolve to desert what was left of his army and return to France. It was now the summer of 1799, and the war news from Europe was disastrous. Bonaparte used this as his excuse for flight, though he really saw it as his opportunity to "rescue" France and ascend the ladder of power still further, wiping out the failure of his Egyptian expedition in the process. On 11 August he summoned his generals and raged for an hour about the idiocy and cowardice of the Directors. It was imperative that he return and prevent the Allies of the Second Coalition from invading France. This was the first of his prepared tirades, and it worked: they agreed he must go. A week later, Admiral Gantaume, commanding the frigates *Muiron* and *Carrière,* told him it was now reasonably safe to put to sea for France, and off he went, leaving Jean-Baptiste Kléber in charge of the doomed army. The latter's comment summed it up: "He had left us *avec ses culottes plein de merde.*" Kléber said he would "go back to France and wipe his face in it."

As it happens, Bonaparte's Egyptian expedition is now remembered not so much for military defeat as for cultural success. Indeed, it had a huge impact in France at the time as the "discovery of the Orient," among a people who, then as now, are either *amateurs d'art*, intellectuals, or at least pseudo-intellectuals. Despite appalling hardships, the cultural experts did their work well. Among other things, they unearthed the Rosetta stone (promptly captured by the British), which, with its trilingual inscription, enabled Jean-François Champollion (assisted by the Englishman Smith) to decode the language of hieroglyphs, a mystery for two millennia. The most enterprising of the experts was the artist-engraver Vivant Denon (1747–1825), a former minor aristocrat and diplomat, who at Naples under the ancien régime had sketched Sir William Hamilton, the British consul in Naples, and his beautiful and notorious wife, Emma, and learned to detest the English. The painter David had brought him forward, and in Egypt he came into his own. He embraced the art and architecture of ancient Egypt with passion, traveling up the Nile with General Louis Desaix, who not only won three brilliant battles but enabled Denon to sketch and subsequently to engrave some of the most remarkable temples. His 150 drawings formed the basis both for his quick-sale *Voyages dans la Basse et la Haute*

Egypte (1802), the first serious description of the civilization of ancient Egypt, and the twenty-four magnificent and sumptuously illustrated volumes of his *Description de l'Egypte*, perhaps the most remarkable publication since the Complutensian Polyglot Bible, a triumph of Spanish sixteenth-century printing in five ancient languages. It is easily the greatest single artifact produced during the entire Napoleonic epoch (though it is rivaled by the Egyptian dinner service made by Sèvres, now in Apsley House, London). These volumes began to appear, with Bonaparte's enthusiastic support, in 1809, and the series was completed in 1828. Denon launched both the Egyptian Revival in Paris and the idea of Bonaparte as a cultural prince-innovator, turning him into a quasi-Renaissance figure with wide appeal not only throughout France but in the whole of Europe. In short, Denon was a propagandist of genius, and Bonaparte made increasing use of his services, as head of the Louvre (soon renamed the Musée Napoléon) and of all France's state museums, to the embellishment of which Denon was appointed licensed looter of all Europe's royal and ecclesiastical art collections.

Bonaparte thus returned to France with a new role as culture hero ahead of him. With his usual luck he evaded Nelson again, and traveled from the south coast to Paris with such speed that he reached the capital before the Directors knew he was back in France (16 October 1799). His reception was enthusiastic and confirmed his view of the French, and especially the Parisians, first formed during the Revolution—that they were volatile and frivolous, with a short attention span, and could easily be diverted from serious misfortunes by transient excitement. He found that his reverses had been forgotten, his successes remembered, and that he was now widely regarded as *l'homme providentiel* who would rescue France from the follies of the Directors.

These follies were economic rather than military, since even before Bonaparte returned to France the generals—chiefly Michel Ney, André Masséna, and Guillaume Brune—had restored the situation on France's frontiers. But inflation soared uncontrollably. The Directory's paper currency, originally traded at fifty francs to the gold franc, had sunk to 100,000. The distress this caused was compounded by a new conscription law that made all five Directors, notably Barras, the most powerful, personal objects of hatred. There were serious food shortages and universal accusations of corruption. Of the Directors, the abbé Joseph Sieyès (1748–1836), an old Revolutionary hand who had helped to sink, in turn, Danton and Robespierre, decided to make himself popular by betraying his colleagues. He recruited Charles-Maurice Talleyrand (1754–1848), who was running foreign policy, and Joseph Fouché (1759–1820), the minister of police, and the three picked Bonaparte as the most likely "sword," who could direct the more forceful side of the business. Even by the sordid standards of Revolution coups, the 18 Brumaire coup (9 November 1799) was a low business, since everyone involved was prepared to betray all the others, and not one of them stuck to what he had sworn to do. If Bonaparte became a ruler of exceptional treachery and mendacity, it must be remembered that he emerged from a political background where a man's word meant nothing, honor was dead, and murder was routine. The coup was preceded by a decree making Bonaparte commander of all troops in the Paris area, including the bodyguard of the Directors. After that, the Directors, including Barras, Bonaparte's mentor and patron, and their 500 elders (a rubber-stamp senate), deputies, and assorted creatures of the pseudodemocratic government were easy meat. The only scene of note was Bonaparte's appearance, in full uniform, accompanied by two grenadiers (leaving the rest of his escort outside) in the actual chamber of the 500 at Saint-Cloud. He was greeted with cries of "Outlaw!" and "Kill him." The grenadiers were beaten and Bonaparte was "shaken like a rat"—the only time in his entire career when hands were laid on his person. At that point the army rushed in and took Bonaparte away, blood covering his face—an uncovenanted accident of which he made the most: "There are men armed with knives, in the pay of England, who are inside the chamber." All the legislators were then put under arrest, and orders were issued for a new constitution to be prepared.

This new constitution, promulgated on 13 December 1799, following a plebiscite, dissolved the Directory and its appendages, and set up, in Roman fashion, a Consulate. The First Consul was Bonaparte, the others being Sieyès and a succession of nonentities. There were also various bodies, the *Conseil d'état, le Tribunat*, the *Corps législatif, le Sénat conservateur*, designed to maintain a representative façade. But in fact what emerged was a simple military dictatorship of one man. The electorate was smaller than the one that produced the *tiers état* or lower house under the ancien régime, the restraints on the executive were far weaker—nonexistent in practice—and the executive itself was personalized in the First Consul to an extent unknown since Louis XIV's time, when he proclaimed: *"L'état—c'est moi."* In fact the new First Consul was far more powerful than Louis XIV, since he dominated the armed forces directly in a country that was now organized as a military state. All the ancient legal restraints on divine-right kingship—the church, the aristocracy and its resources, the courts, the cities and their charters, the universities and their privileges, the guilds and their immunities—all had already been swept away by the Revolution, leaving France a legal blank on which Bonaparte could stamp the irresistible force of his personality. After this one coup, it was easy for Bonaparte to make himself Consul for Life (4 August 1802) and in due course emperor (18 May 1804).

But first he had to justify his vast power by a personal military victory at the head of his armies. The elites and the people had promoted the Man on Horseback to impose order after the years of revolution and tumult, but now they expected him to scatter their enemies. The Austrians, during his absence, had reconquered most of north Italy, thus nullifying his earlier campaign there and upsetting his peace of Campo Formio. So Italy was the natural battleground for him. He spent the early months of 1800 reorganizing the army, then personally led a great set-piece prelude to his campaign by taking an army of 50,000, himself at its head, through the Great Saint Bernard Pass at a time of year (the third week of May) when conditions were still icy and the snow deep. This produced the finest of all Napoleonic images, captured by David, of the Man on Horseback urging on his troops amid the snow. In fact he ascended the Alps on a tiresome mule, which he cursed and belabored as it slithered on the ice, but he did get his men safely across, though they lost much of their heavy equipment in the passage. He gloated: "We have fallen on the Austrians like a thunderbolt!"

This second Italian campaign was full of risks and near disasters, and its culminating battle at Marengo (14 June 1800), where Bonaparte was short of artillery and had only 24,000 men facing a much larger Austrian force, nearly went against him. He was saved by his favorite general, Desaix, who made it possible for Bonaparte to launch a surprising counter-attack after nearly fourteen hours' hard fighting, and it was this which tumbled the Austrians into a scramble for safety, having lost 14,000 men. Desaix was killed in the moment of triumph, evoking from Bonaparte a rare personal tribute. Marengo was presented as one of Bonaparte's most spectacular victories, but it was a close-run thing that might have gone either way. Nor did it end the war, which dragged on throughout the summer and autumn until another French army destroyed the main Austrian force at Hohenlinden (3 December), leaving Vienna naked. The Treaty of Lunéville (February 1801) followed, Austria being forced to acknowledge the creation of various French satellites in Holland, Germany, and Italy, and to allow France the Rhine as her eastern border. Bonaparte took full credit for this peace, soon followed by the Peace of Amiens with the English. His consulate for life was the reward.

In the meantime, Bonaparte had severed himself from his Revolutionary past by an act of statesmanship that long outlived him. Not only had he no religious belief, he actively disliked clerics, except his useful Corsican uncle, Cardinal Fesch. But he recognized that most French people were Catholics and would remain so. The outlawing and persecution of the French church made no sense to him. A persecuted church was a focus and excuse for civil unrest in Catholic France, especially in the southwest, Brittany, and Alsace-Lorraine. Then again, he thought that the clergy made admirable schoolteachers, at least in primary schools, instilling in their young pupils simple morals and a respect for duly constituted authority. Moreover, by making peace with the church, he prepared the way for a reconciliation with the old landowners and aristocrats who had been driven into exile by the Revolution, and whom he wanted back to provide further legitimacy to his regime. Bonaparte in 1800 saw endless vistas opening up before him as the first ruler of Europe. But they demanded, for realization, a France united behind his leadership, or as united as he could make it.

Hence in 1801–2 he negotiated and had passed into law a concordat with Pope Pius VII. It reversed Revolutionary laws passed in the 1790s and reestablished Catholicism as the religion "of the majority of the French." In some respects it went back to the earlier concordat of Leo X and François I (1516), which allowed the French government to supervise the appointment of the higher clergy and the payment of the lower ones. It lasted until 1905, when it fell victim to the anticlerical backlash following the Dreyfus case, and can be regarded as Bonaparte's most durable civil achievement next to his law code. It incorporated an agreement establishing relations between France and the papacy, thus making Pius VII available to sanction Bonaparte's acceptance of a crown and to preside at a coronation.

The actual enthronement of Bonaparte, which was clearly coming, was precipitated by the so-called Pichegru-Cadoudal plot, which came to light in November 1803. It involved General Victor Moreau (a rival military hero and the victor of Hohenlinden), the British secret service, and Georges Cadoudal (leader of the Chouan rebels of Brittany), and it proposed to kill Bonaparte and replace him by a new consulate. The plotters were variously disposed of, and in the process Bonaparte had the young duc d'Enghien, a minor royal, abducted from Germany and judicially murdered. Enghien was probably innocent and certainly harmless, and his killing was designed to inspire terror among more dangerous exiles. It was now widely proposed, no doubt at Bonaparte's direction, that he be declared emperor, on the grounds that a hereditary succession would confirm and perpetuate the regime and make his assassination pointless. On 4 May, the Senate proposed and passed a resolution making Bonaparte hereditary "Emperor of the French," with the title of Napoleon I. On 14 May, a new constitution was published. It was confirmed by plebiscite on 6 November, with 3,571,329 "yes" votes to 2,570 "noes." (Bonaparte was the first dictator to produce fake election figures.) Bonaparte was entitled by law to nominate his own successor, if necessary an adopted son. A coronation was staged at Notre Dame on 2 December 1804. The décor was gilt, the image a golden bee. The pope was present, having been kept waiting for four hours in a freezing cathedral before being denied his real role in the ceremony, since Bonaparte himself took the crowns from the altar and placed them on his own head and Josephine's. There is some dispute whether this gesture was spontaneous or rehearsed and had been cleared with the pope. The ceremony was marred by rows between Josephine and Bonaparte's sisters, who hated her and resented being told to carry her train. She burst into tears when the crown was put on her head and later complained of agony when she was made to continue wearing it all through the protracted coronation feast that followed. So far as can be seen, the assumption of the crown made no difference either way in effecting a reconciliation between the regime and royalist exiles, or in getting the courts of Europe to accept the legitimacy of Napoleonic rule in their hearts as opposed to treaties won in battle. Becoming emperor lost Bonaparte most of the European liberals. But it increased his power over the army, especially over the rank and file. It became the foundation stone of a mounting edifice of satellite kingdoms, princedoms, and duchies, of medals, honors, and stars, of protocols and privileges that the new emperor created and bestowed at will, and frequently revoked, too. But behind the tinsel and the glitter, Bonaparte was still only as secure as his last victory made him.

CHAPTER THREE

The Master of the Battlefield

BONAPARTE WAS FIRST and foremost a military man, a soldier, a general, a commander of armies, and a deadly destroyer of his opponents' military capacity. His aim throughout his career was to move swiftly to a position where he obliged the enemy to fight a major battle, destroy the enemy's forces, and then occupy his capital and dictate peace terms. That is what he invariably did when he had any choice in the matter. He was absolutely consistent in his grand strategy, and on the whole it served him well. It fitted his temperament, which was audacious, hyperactive, aggressive, and impatient of results. Indeed, impatience was his salient characteristic, serving him for both good and ill. As Wellington, who thoroughly understood Bonaparte's strengths and weaknesses, remarked, he lacked the patience to fight a defensive campaign, and even when he appeared to be doing so, in the winter of 1813–14, he was really looking for an opportunity to make an attack and win a decisive, aggressive battle.

Hence speed was of the essence in Bonaparte's methods. He used speed both to secure the maximum disparity between his own forces and the enemy's, by attacking the latter before they were fully mobilized and deployed, and also to secure surprise, both strategic and tactical. He moved large armies

across Europe faster than any man before him. He was abl
do this, first, because of his ability to read both large- and sma
scale maps and plan the fastest and safest routes. In the study
of terrain, and the visual reconstruction of it in his own mind,
his imagination was at its most potent. Second, helped by
good staff officers, he was able to translate these campaign
routes into detailed orders for all arms with a celerity and ex-
actitude that were truly astonishing. Third, he infused all his
commanders with this appetite for speed and fast movement.
Indeed, the common soldiers learned to move fast, taking long
marches for granted in the knowledge that, whenever possible,
Bonaparte tried to ensure they got lifts on baggage carts in ro-
tation. (During the Hundred Days he got his troops to Paris
without obliging most of them to march at all.)

Bonaparte himself set an example of speed. He was often
seen flogging not only his own horse but that of his aide riding alongside him. His consumption of horsepower was un-
precedented and horrifying. In the pursuit of speed by his
armies, hundreds of thousands of these creatures died in their
traces, driven beyond endurance. Millions of them died during his wars, and the struggle to replace them became one of
his most formidable supply problems. The quality of French
remounts deteriorated steadily during the decade 1805–15
and this helps to explain the declining performance of the
French cavalry.

The speed with which his armies moved was also due to
the strong motivation of his troops. The armies identified their
interests and their future with Bonaparte, and the lower the
rank, the more complete this identification became. There is

a puzzle here. Bonaparte cared nothing for the lives of his soldiers. He disregarded losses, provided his objectives were secured. He told Metternich in 1813, during a day-long argument about the future of Europe, that he would gladly sacrifice a million men to secure his paramountcy. Moreover, having got his army into a fix, and having written off the campaign accordingly, he repeatedly abandoned the army to its fate and hastened back to Paris to secure his political position. This happened in Egypt, in Russia, in Spain, and in Germany. Bonaparte was never held to account for these desertions, or indeed for his losses of French troops, which averaged more than 50,000 killed a year. By comparison, Wellington's losses from his six years' campaign in the Iberian Peninsula totaled 36,000 from all causes, including desertion, or 6,000 a year. This disparity brought a rueful reflection from Wellington:

> I can hardly conceive of anything greater than Napoleon at the head of an army—especially a French army. Then he had one prodigious advantage—he had no responsibility—he could do what he pleased; and no man ever lost more armies than he did. Now with me the loss of every man told. I could not risk so much. I knew that if I ever lost 500 men without the clearest necessity, I should be brought on my knees to the bar of the House of Commons.

This freedom to take risks, which Bonaparte enjoyed except at the outset of his career, was not enjoyed by any of his opponents, all of whom were surrounded by jealous rivals and subject to political authority. And Bonaparte took the fullest possible advantage of it throughout. It fit in perfectly with his general strategy of swift aggression and offensive battle seeking. It usually came off, and when it did not, Bonaparte gave practical expression to the old army maxim "never reinforce failure," and left.

The soldiers liked this high-risk approach. In their calculations, they were as likely to be killed by a defensive and cautious commander as by an attacking one, and with little chance of loot to balance the risk. Soldiers like action. High casualty rates mean quicker promotion and higher pay. Moreover, in Bonaparte's armies, unlike all the others, promotion was usually on merit. Private soldiers had a good chance of promotion to senior noncommissioned rank and a reasonable chance of becoming officers, even generals. Under Bonaparte's rules, a proficient soldier could transfer to the Guard, the army's elite force, where he was paid as much as a sergeant in a line regiment. Good food (where possible), high rates of pay, and loot—these were the material inducements Bonaparte offered. He also fraternized with the men. Byron's friend Hobhouse, who watched Bonaparte inspect a parade during the Hundred Days, was astonished to see him pull the noses of soldiers he picked out from the ranks. This was taken as a sign of affection. He also slapped the faces of favored officers, quite hard. This, too, was not taken amiss. Bonaparte knew how to talk to his men around their campfires. His public addresses were short and simple: "Soldiers, I expect you to fight hard today." "Soldiers, be brave, be resolute!" "Soldiers, make me proud of you!" Bonaparte liked and expected to be cheered by his men, in contrast to Wellington, who dismissed cheering as "coming dangerously close to an expression of opinion," and would never have dreamed of touching one of his officers, let alone a private soldier; he detested commissioning from the ranks, believing that officers so made remained slaves to drink. There were advantages and disadvantages to both approaches.

Once Bonaparte became First Consul, and still more after he was crowned, he turned his soldiers into a privileged caste. Wellington often observed that Bonaparte's presence on the field was worth 40,000 men in the balance. What he meant was not a tribute to Bonaparte's tactical skill but a reflection on his power. He explained his remark in a memorandum he wrote for Lord Stanhope in 1836:

[Napoleon] was the sovereign of the country as well as the chief of the army. That country was constituted on a military basis. All its institutions were framed for the purpose of forming and maintaining its armies with a view to conquest. All the offices and rewards of the state were reserved in the first instance exclusively for the army. An officer, even a private soldier, of the army might look to the sovereignty of a kingdom as the reward for his services. It is obvious that the presence of the sovereign with an army so constituted must greatly excite their exertions.

Wellington added that all the resources of the French state were directed to the particular operation Bonaparte commanded to give it the maximum chance of success. He enjoyed direct, not delegated power like most commanders in chief, and to a degree, Wellington said, never before exercised by a sovereign in the field. He made all his subordinate appointments according to his own notions, without the need to consult anyone. (Wellington, by contrast, often had generals foisted upon him by the Horse Guards and sometimes could not even choose his own staff officers.) Finally, Wellington thought, Bonaparte's sovereignty stilled disputes among his marshals and thus gave the French army "a unity of action."

Wellington might have made a further point. Bonaparte also controlled all the domestic channels of communication, including a subservient press. He could thus, except in extremis, present his own version of military events, and the roles played in them by individuals and units, to the French public and the world. He was not the first sovereign–commander in chief to appreciate the uses of propaganda, but certainly the first to recognize its central importance in war, and to take full advantage of the increasingly large-scale media, from giant placards to steam-produced newspapers, now available. The state semaphore and posting systems meant that he could always get his version to Paris first, and this enabled him, for instance, to present his Egyptian expedition as a huge cultural success, rather than a complete naval and military failure. He could also, if necessary, manipulate the mob, in much the same way as Arab military dictators do it in our time—not through a state political party, as in their case, but through the structures of the National Guard and other paramilitary formations that survived from Revolutionary times and remained loyal to him. Bonaparte had lived through the old times when civilian mobs intimidated the royal soldiers and persuaded them to be disloyal. Now he reversed the process—it was the military who set the political tone and the civilians who followed them.

The French nation was behind the army during the Napoleonic period (1800–14), in a way that would not have been possible in any other European country at that time. The army was the premier institution of the state—in a sense it almost *was* the state—and the soldiers knew it. It made them proud and bolstered their morale. Here was one of the keys to Bonaparte's military success: he could draw on this morale, rely on it, exploit it, before it was eventually destroyed, in Spain and Russia. The French army, under Bonaparte at his best, had an enviable corporate arrogance. It knew it was the finest. Correspondingly, it inspired fear, except among the best professional troops, and sometimes even among them.

Indeed, fear was Bonaparte's most useful weapon. It was the one he employed most frequently. In his aggressive strategy, it gave him a head start—it was as though an invisible army had softened up the enemy's defenses before a French shot was fired. During his campaigns, with few exceptions, Bonaparte faced coalitions of nations with vastly superior manpower resources, if properly assembled and deployed. His strategy therefore was not only to strike quickly but to strike between his opponents' forces, before they could join together. He went for each in turn, hoping he would have numerical superiority and defeat them separately. The Allied armies thus rarely had the confidence of numbers, and even when they had, Bonaparte's notorious ability to bring up reinforcements quickly and surprisingly tended to undermine it.

Granted these initial advantages, Bonaparte's battle tactics were usually simple. Of course he knew of all the classic dodges—encirclement, attack from the rear, ambush—and used them when opportunity presented. His understanding and exploitation of terrain was comprehensive. Whenever possible, he deliberately chose his battlefields. But once his army was deployed on ground of his choosing, he simply attacked. His tactics were all of a piece with his strategy. There was much sense in this policy. In early nineteenth-century warfare, with unarmored men exposed to cannon and shot, it was essential to morale for a unit to keep in tight formation. Once that was lost, it was likely it would disintegrate into a shambles and run. No matter how well drilled and disciplined, a unit was likely to lose formation if ordered to carry out complicated movements over distances. Hence the simpler the plan the better, and the simplest plan was: attack!

Moreover, the French army under Bonaparte was trained and organized for attack, and it had the equipment and formations to do so effectively. A good staff and reliable field signaling systems, expertly organized by General Berthier, meant that attacks were well timed and coordinated. There was no set procedure, but it was usually as follows. First, an intense artillery barrage. Bonaparte had good guns, plenty of them, and good gunners. His horse artillery could maneuver its teams to within close reach of the enemy, so the cannon could be fired point-blank, thus trebling the rate of fire. Then they could be whisked away if enemy cavalry tried to overrun them. The proper response to the barrage was to dig shallow slit trenches, but this meant carrying spades, and they were not usually available. The alternative, which Wellington stumbled on early in the peninsular campaign, and therefore employed whenever he could, was to command the infantry to lie down, especially on a reverse slope (if available). This cut casualties to virtually nil and taught the infantry they had nothing to fear from the French guns. But Austrian, Prussian, and Russian commanders never adopted this tactic, fearing loss of formation. At all events, Bonaparte's opening barrages usually had considerable effect, inflicting heavy casualties and inspiring yet more fear.

Behind the guns were the cavalry, waiting for the barrage to cease, reconnoitering the weak spots in the enemy line, and charging when appropriate. Bonaparte had by far the best cavalry in Europe, as Wellington acknowledged (his own he considered brave but unbiddable, and often positively dangerous to their own side). They had the great advantage that they could conduct a limited charge—that is, overrun a position and then re-form, instead of individually pursuing fleeing soldiers. The discipline of the French cavalry was due largely to some outstanding commanders, notably Masséna and Murat. But there were many others. The French cavalry were originally fairly well mounted, but after about 1808 the quality of horses declined and this was reflected in the cavalry's loss of panache and power of impact.

Bonaparte was not so foolish as to suppose that victory against a determined professional enemy could be secured by guns and cavalry alone. The infantry were essential to master and retain the field. They, too, were trained to inspire fear, advancing at the rapid *pas de charge,* with drums beating ferociously, bugles blaring, and trained war cries. Bonaparte exploited the intimidating power of martial noise, and he reinforced this with the design of uniforms intended to make his infantry seem taller. This was particularly true of the Old Guard, chosen for height anyway but made more formidable by huge bearskins sometimes two feet high. (The Old Guard had at least five year's experience; the Young Guard were the best of each year's conscripts.) The total Guard numbered 50,000 and formed a separate army in itself (rather like Hitler's military SS divisions). They were kept behind the line regiments and deployed so that they could be sent to any part of the battle when needed. Their presence was a comfort to the line, and if the line did its job well, they did not need to be thrown into action at all. Thus, paradoxically, the elite Guard, especially the Old Guard, the best troops, saw less action than most units, unlike the British guards, who were always in the thick of it. This could have serious consequences. The Old Guard failed Bonaparte at Waterloo, when they were most needed.

Bonaparte, having completed his three-wave attack, then reassessed the tactical situation and took measures accordingly. He directed operations from a piece of high ground or the roof of a building, if available. Sometimes he had a scaffolding tower made. But this was dangerous, and Bonaparte, though unquestionably brave, did not take needless risks with his person. He dressed in the dark green underuniform of the chasseurs of the Guard, sometimes with a gray greatcoat over it, which was inconspicuous. He never wore decorations in action (it was the flashing stars Nelson invariably wore on the quarterdeck that attracted the French sniper's attention at Trafalgar and killed him). Wellington followed the same routine, wearing a dark suit almost indistinguishable from civilian dress. But whereas Bonaparte wore his hat square on, Wellington put the ends fore and aft. Why? Wellington liked to raise his hat, out of courtesy and to return salutes. Bonaparte rarely raised his hat to anyone.

Both used telescopes constantly. Bonaparte often criticized the French optical industry for not producing better models. It was notorious that British officers had superior ones, and the first act of a French officer when dealing with a British prisoner of rank was to relieve him of his telescope.

Directing a major battle in the poor visibility caused by drifting gunsmoke was no easy matter. Most of the Napoleonic battle pictures were painted long after the event by artists who were not present, and they drastically simplified the scene. But at Aspern, the battle was drawn while it was actually taking place by a professional Austrian watercolorist who was perched high on a building from which he could survey most of the field. His work's verisimilitude leaves an impression of great confusion. No wonder experienced generals favored simple plans. Issuing fresh orders was not easy. They usually had to be carried by the hand of a brave and reliable aide-de-camp. Berthier, as staff chief, always sent more than one officer with duplicate orders—sometimes a dozen if the distance was great. But this was a military luxury of the kind that Bonaparte, who could command virtually unlimited resources, usually enjoyed. In any case, toward the end of a battle, the supply of ADCs ran out. All kinds of people were roped in to carry scraps of paper. At Waterloo, Wellington discovered a patriotic English tourist, who had somehow got involved in the battle, and made good use of him as a messenger. But often a commanding general had to ride about the battlefield and give orders in person. That was often how he was killed or captured.

Though Bonaparte was an exceptionally enterprising and aggressive strategist and tactician, he was in many ways a rather conservative military man. Most of the military innovations from which he benefited—the general staff, the new artillery, the semaphore, and so on—had been introduced under the ancien régime or during the Revolutionary period. The French state had magnificent arsenals and arms factories, but Bonaparte never set up a department to study and make use of scientific warfare or new technology—this despite his frequent and public commendation of the scientific approach. France had many skilled engineers, chemists, physicists, and biologists who might have been put to military use. The American naval engineer and inventor Robert Fulton, who built the first steamship and who was fiercely anti-British, appeared in France with all kinds of ideas, especially for submarines. But he got only lukewarm support from the French admiralty and none from Bonaparte himself. It was left to a British colonel, Henry Shrapnel, to invent what was to become for generations the most effective antipersonnel shell, and to the Royal Ordnance at Woolwich to start work on rockets.

Bonaparte enjoyed the services of a military scientist of genius in the shape of Domenique-Jean Larrey, who devoted his life to military medicine and was with Bonaparte on some of his most arduous campaigns. It was Larrey who invented the Flying Ambulance, the first effective vehicle for getting the wounded rapidly off the field. This was part of a system Larrey designed for ensuring that as many casualties as possible received proper medical treatment as quickly as possible. It undoubtedly worked, and saved innumerable lives. Moreover, Larrey deprecated the atrocious habit of military surgeons of sawing off arms and legs on the slightest pretext, usually because a bullet, in entering the limb, had carried with it a portion of clothing so that the wound became infected. He thought that limbs could usually be saved, and proved it in many cases.

Yet curiously enough, though Bonaparte lavished praise on Larrey's skills and character, he never made him head of the army's medical services. The post went instead to an older and more conservative man, Pierre-François Percy, who was surgeon in chief to the army, later the Grande Armée, from 1801 to 1812, when he retired. (The Grande Armée was introduced in 1805, meaning the Imperial Army when formed into a single body for a major campaign.) Larrey then indeed succeeded him for a time, but when Bonaparte returned from Elba he reappointed Percy, who by then was clearly past it. For most of the wars, Larrey had to be content to be chief surgeon to the Guard, who thought the world of his methods. Bonaparte only once employed him personally. He preferred Alexandre Yvan, who served him from 1796 to 1814. The reason was that Yvan held old-fashioned views on amputation and the use of the scalpel as opposed to time, nursing, and medications. Bonaparte preferred the risk of losing a limb to the possible alternative of putrefaction and death. The same reasoning seems to have applied to his preference for Percy, an old hacksaw-and-chopper man. We have here a clue to an important element in Bonaparte's personality. Like many people—most people, probably—who are radical and "progressive" in general, he tended to be conservative in particular, especially on matters he thought he knew a lot about. Battle wounds were one of these subjects. Another was cannon and ammunition. On these matters he thought the improvements introduced in his youth were quite enough, and though he fiddled with the standard equipment, he never changed it substantially. Pontoons, mobile metal bridging materials, siege howitzers, anything involving naval technology including barges and troopships—he was not interested. He made little use of observation balloons; indeed he took no notice of airpower, though it was then much discussed. He ignored steam power, though the traction engine and the railroad were just over the horizon, and rail was to transform grand strategy in the decades to come. One might have said that the military rail was made for Bonaparte's geostrategy of swift transfer of armies. But he preferred merely to improve the old military road system, mostly laid down in the days of Louis XIV. It is a fact that Bonaparte introduced many innovations, notably the decimal system. But he was never keen on decimals, preferring the old system in which he had shone in youth, and on Saint Helena he denounced it root and branch. Radical in appearance, he had a hard, obstinate, conservative core.

One suspects that Bonaparte would have subscribed to the modern American adage "If it ain't broke, don't fix it."

What he inherited, he improved and built upon, but he was disinclined to change a military apparatus that worked well for him. And he had reason for complacency. His record as a battle winner and conqueror, as a destroyer of armies and subjugator of governments, has never been equaled. Or rather, one has to go back to Alexander the Great to find comparable success. It may be useful at this stage to summarize his wars and campaigns, the coalitions that resisted him, and how he dealt with them.

The First Coalition of 1792–97 came into existence as a result of the French invasion of the Austrian Netherlands. The French government declared war against the Austrian emperor in his capacity of king of Hungary, hoping that Austria's defensive treaties would not thereby be invoked. In fact the coalition was swiftly formed, involving Austria, Prussia, Britain (from 1793), Naples, Portugal, Spain, Sweden, and various smaller states. The coalition was never cohesive, and in 1795 Tuscany, Prussia, Luxembourg, Sweden, and Spain defected, making separate peace treaties. Bonaparte came onto the scene in a leading role in 1797, and as a result of his Italian victories, he forced the Austrians to sign preliminary terms at Leoben on 17 April 1797, confirmed by the Treaty of Campo Formio in October.

Britain, which had won naval victories and taken French overseas possessions, refused French terms, continued the struggle, and tried to form the Second Coalition. Britain had already begun the system of financing coalition partners in Naples, and these were on offer from 1798 onward, the British naval victory against Bonaparte's fleet at the Battle of the Nile providing further encouragement. Naples was the first to join Britain, followed by other Italian states and Austria (Prussia remaining benevolently neutral), and by Russia and Turkey, which took action against the French occupation of the Ionian Isles. But the Austrians lost the Italian campaign, Bonaparte marching the Reserve Army through the Saint Bernard Pass to take them in the rear and win the decisive Battle of Marengo (14 June 1800). In November, though detained himself in Paris to consolidate his political position, he directed a vigorous campaign against Austria in Germany, culminating in the victory of Hohenlinden (3 December). Austria made peace at the Treaty of Lunéville in February 1801. William Pitt, British prime minister and Bonaparte's most vigorous and consistent opponent, resigned the same month. By now Portugal was Britain's only ally, so the coalition was effectively dead, and Pitt's successor, Henry Addington, made a preliminary peace at Amiens in October 1801. This was the only interruption in Britain's war against France from 1793 to 1814.

Nor did it last long. Both Britain and France, mutually suspicious, refused to carry out the terms of the treaty. Each accused the other of bad faith. In February 1803, Bonaparte summoned Lord Whitworth, the British ambassador and an old-fashioned gentleman-diplomat, to a stormy interview. Whitworth was barely allowed to speak, and he judged the object of the meeting was "to frighten and to bully." He reported that "such conduct in private life would be a strong presumption of weakness," and that was the conclusion he drew from the tirade. He haughtily added that one expression

Bonaparte used "was too trivial and vulgar to find a place in a dispatch, or anywhere but in the mouth of a hackney coachman." A month later, on 13 March, Bonaparte reenacted the scene at a public diplomatic reception in the Tuileries. Whitworth was a big, imposing man, and his mere size, self-control, and taciturnity infuriated Bonaparte. Going up to Whitworth, Bonaparte accused Britain, in a loud voice, which could be heard by all the guests, of planning war for another fifteen years. He then added, "The English don't respect treaties. So we will cover them in mourning." Then he left the room so fast that the flunkies did not have time to open the double doors, and he stood fuming for a second while they fiddled with the knobs.

This was the kind of violent outburst that Hitler was later to make his speciality, to terrify those he addressed and to spread fear among onlookers. But whereas Hitler's rages were deliberate and rehearsed, Bonaparte sometimes lost his temper, and usually regretted it, as on this occasion. But it made little difference anyway. Britain and Bonaparte were again at war from May 1803, and it was during this period that a French invasion of Britain became a serious possibility. Flat-bottomed boats were collected in French Channel ports, soldiers encamped. The British took the threat with gravity and made intense preparations, including building a fortress in the Midlands in which it was planned to place the king and his government in the event of a French landing and occupation of London. But no detailed plans for transshipment of troops and an opposed landing have survived, and it is possible none were made. Bonaparte hated the idea of sea warfare

and shuddered at the idea of participating in it. Yet for anyone else to lead the invasion would have invoked odious comparisons with Caesar's invasion of Britain. Bonaparte talked specifically of what he would do in London, mentioning a seizure of the Bank of England and the appropriation of its fabulous gold reserves. But by comparison with the eagerness with which he seized on opportunities for land offensives on the largest scale, and the rapidity with which he executed them, his slow and hesitant approach to invading Britain is significant—his heart was never in it. And Nelson's spectacular victory at Trafalgar on 21 October 1805 put an end to any possibility of invasion.

By that time Pitt had returned to office in 1804 and immediately set about putting together the Third Coalition, centering around a Russian-Austrian alliance, the arrangement being completed on 9 August 1805. The British provided more than £12 million in subsidies and agreed with Sweden to land troops in northern Germany, and this led Prussia to join the coalition in the autumn. The central idea was an Austrian invasion of France supported by 250,000 Russian troops. But Bonaparte swiftly abandoned his English invasion plans and moved large quantities of troops (of what was now renamed the Grande Armée) into Italy and Germany. The speed with which he acted contrasted sharply with the sluggishness of Austrian and, still more, Russian movements. One Austrian army in Bavaria was surrounded at Ulm and surrendered on 20 October. Bonaparte himself took charge of the French troops now operating in Austria against the main armies of Russia and Austria, which had finally joined forces

under the personal command of their two emperors. By a series of ruses, including skillful concealment of the strength of
his army, Bonaparte succeeded in enticing the emperors to
give him battle at Austerlitz on 2 December.

This famous battle, generally regarded as Bonaparte's
most brilliant victory, took place in atrocious winter conditions of cold, fog, frozen but treacherous ponds, snow, and
ice, over rugged country that ranged from rocks to marsh.
The combined Austrian and Russian strength was about
90,000 men, with 280 guns. Bonaparte had 73,000 men and
139 guns, but his ruses persuaded the Allied command that
he had no more than 40,000. Believing they outnumbered
Bonaparte by more than two to one, they were happy to see
him take up a defensive position. He thus had the ground of
his choosing, and it was well chosen. But although, contrary
to his usual practice, he invited initial attack, he was prepared
and able to launch both cavalry and infantry attacks of his
own, and this was his response after the initial Russian and
Austrian forward movements revealed an absence of determination and a confusion of plan.

The battle began at eight A.M., when it was still dark, and
it was virtually over by early afternoon, with the Allied forces
separated and retreating in different directions. Bonaparte tri-
umphed for three reasons. First, he had complete unity of
command. The senior Allied commander, M. I. Kutuzov, had
in practice no chance to adopt and carry out a unified tactical
plan, and authority was hopelessly divided between sovereigns and individual commanders, some of whom acted on
their own initiative. Second, in the poor conditions, orders

frequently miscarried or were misunderstood or disobeyed. Both sides were affected by this, but the French much less so, since Bonaparte knew exactly what he was doing and his only problem was getting his commanders to obey his orders quickly and in full. Although in the battle he destroyed both the armies facing him as fighting units, he proclaimed loudly after the event that if his generals had been more prompt, the Austrian-Russian forces would have been annihilated. As it was, the Allies lost 27,000, including prisoners, against French losses of 9,000, most of them wounded. Third, French units operated more efficiently. Their cavalry repeatedly attacked and dispersed superior numbers of Allied cavalry, and the artillery were persistently resourceful: informed that the Russians were trying to escape over frozen ponds, they quickly prepared red-hot shot and fired them into the ice, breaking it and causing 2,000 Russians to be drowned. The infantry of the lines were so effective that Bonaparte did not have to call on the Guard at all.

Austerlitz ended the Third Coalition, the Austrian emperor, who had had enough of active campaigning, suing for terms the very next day. The Peace of Pressburg was agreed to at the end of the month. Pitt (who, on hearing the news of Austerlitz, had despairingly cried: "Roll up the map of Europe—we shall not be needing it this many a long year!") died early in 1806. But subsequent British peace feelers came to nothing, and the Fourth Coalition emerged after Prussia declared war in August 1806. Bonaparte was reluctant to go to war because he sensed weariness of the endless conflict in France, but once he gathered his 150,000-strong army and marched it into Germany, using forest cover to mask its strength, he behaved with characteristic decisiveness and resolution against an enemy that had no real war plan and whose armies, though totaling more than 200,000 men in all, were disjointed and uncoordinated. In a series of engagements, at Saalfeld (19 October), Jena and Auerstadt (14 October), and Lübeck (3 November), he broke up all Prussia's main armies, inflicted 25,000 casualties, took 14,000 prisoners and 2,000 guns, and occupied the Prussian capital, Berlin. With Russian support and British subsidies, Prussia carried on the war through the winter, losing a ferocious encounter with the Grande Armée at Eylau on 8 February 1807 but inflicting heavy losses. The spring brought a respite, while both sides rebuilt their forces. Bonaparte, who had occupied Warsaw, raised a Polish army and called up a new intake of French conscripts a year early, thus raising his total forces to 600,000 men. In June he advanced toward the Prussian king in Königsberg, brought his army to battle at Friedland (14 June), and won a decisive victory, forcing both Prussia and Russia to sign a peace treaty at Tilsit (7 July). This once more left Britain as Bonaparte's sole opponent.

The struggle then switched to Spain, which had been a reluctant French ally, had lost its fleet at Trafalgar—Admiral Nelson's decisive victory over the combined French and Spanish navies on 21 October 1805—and was becoming increasingly nationalist and anti-French. In March 1808, Bonaparte decided on direct invasion and occupation, but a popular rising in Madrid in May began a struggle, in which a British army joined, and which proved increasingly costly for the French. Thus encouraged, Austria, which had stayed out of the Fourth Coalition but had been rearming, decided to go to war against France on 8 February 1809. This is called the war of the Fifth Coalition, though Russia (nominally a French ally) and Prussia did not join it. Large-scale maneuvering in the spring culminated on 22 May in the Battle of Aspern, which was costly and indecisive for the French and is often counted as Bonaparte's first major defeat. However, he reestablished his reputation with a major victory at Wagram on 6 July. On 12 July the Austrian forces signed an armistice, translated into the Treaty of Schönbrun in October 1809. This ended the Fifth Coalition.

So far all the coalitions had failed. Bonaparte's strategy of lightning wars, aimed at bringing his opponents one by one to a large-scale battle, destroying their army, and occupying their capital, then imposing a punitive peace, was a highly successful formula. It directed Bonaparte's great qualities—speed of action, decisiveness, risk taking, and wonderful leadership, together with iron will and courage—with absolute precision to the attaining of his objects. Of course, it could not have succeeded without the corresponding weaknesses of his enemies—lethargy, indecisiveness, and weak, divided leadership, together with a lack of will to see the struggle through, and often blatant cowardice. Their conduct was brilliantly summed up by a British journalist, Leigh Hunt, editor of the *Examiner*, a radical journal that, though fundamentally patriotic and pro-British, was by no means unsympathetic to the French Revolutionary spirit. In his *Autobiography*, he wrote of Austria, Prussia, and Russia (and the lesser Allies) that it was precisely their pygmy behavior that made Bonaparte seem such a giant.

It is a melancholy period for the potentates of the earth when they fancy themselves obliged to resort to the shabbiest measures of the feeble; siding against a friend with the enemy; joining in accusations against him at the latter's dictation; believed by nobody on either side; returning to the friend, and retreating from him, according to the fortunes of war; secretly hoping that the friend will excuse them by reason of the pauper's plea, necessity; and at no time able to give better apologies for their conduct than those "mysterious ordinations of Providence" which are the last refuge of the destitute in morals. . . . Yet this is what the allies of England were in the habit of doing through the whole contest of England with France. When England succeeded in getting up a coalition against Napoleon, they denounced him for his ambition, and set out to fight him. When the coalition was broken by his armies, they turned round at his bidding, denounced England, and joined him in fighting against their ally. And this was the round of their history: a coalition and tergiversation alternately; now a speech and a fight against Bonaparte, who beat them; then a speech and a fight against England, who bought them off; then again a speech and a fight against Bonaparte, who beat them again; and then as before a speech and a fight against England, who again bought them off. Meanwhile they took everything they could get, whether from enemy or friend, seizing with no less greediness whatever bits of territory Bonaparte threw to them for their meanness, then pocketing the millions of Pitt, for which we are paying to this day.

Thus from 1799 to the end of 1809, Bonaparte seemed invincible and strode the landmass of Europe like a colossus. But his position and future were still insecure—he needed a further large-scale triumph. Once his military resources became overstretched, as they did from 1809 onward, and his capacity to deliver set-battle victories ended, as it did from 1810, the coalitions that his overreaching ambition and pride raised against him became far more formidable. The Sixth Coalition was brought into being by Bonaparte's invasion of Russia in 1812, and it worked with increasing resources and success until the defeated emperor abdicated in April 1814, followed by the victorious allied Treaty of Paris. This sent Bonaparte to Elba as a petty ruler, while the Bourbon king, younger brother of the executed Louis XVI, was restored to the old throne as King Louis XVIII. The great powers then gathered in Vienna to devise a lasting settlement of European frontiers, and they were still in congress when Bonaparte escaped from Elba and returned to France. Their reaction to his audacity was swift and purposeful and produced what is sometimes called the Seventh Coalition, an amalgam of all the powers that had ever opposed Bonapartism, and that led directly to Bonaparte's total overthrow at Waterloo.

But that is to anticipate events. What is clear from the story of the seven coalitions is that Bonaparte remained, from start to finish, a military man. As such, he enjoyed extraordinary success. Where he failed was as a politician, and still more as an international statesman. His failure was so complete that it eventually involved his military ruin, too.

CHAPTER FOUR

The Flawed and Fragile Empire

IF THE RECORD shows that Bonaparte was a great general, it equally demonstrates beyond argument that he could not rule on a long-term basis. No one has ever been faster than he was at overturning existing governments, setting up new administrations, and imposing constitutions to fit them. None lasted more than a few years, some only a few months. His empire waxed and waned, but it was throughout in a state of flux. It always bore the hallmarks of his impatience and his lack of tenacity in sustaining the long haul. It is unhistorical to engage in psychological examinations of Bonaparte's character with a view to explaining his successes or failures in the running of nations. But his lack of heirs, and the stability and confidence they provide for a man who had won thrones by his own efforts, clearly contributed to the provisional nature of his imperial administration. If Bonaparte had been married earlier, to a fertile woman, and produced children to succeed and assist him, who could be trained to rule, he would have looked at the empire as a long-term investment to be treated and coaxed and cherished accordingly.

But here we come into unfathomable depths. Bonaparte's emotional and sexual life remains a mystery, despite all that has been written about it. That he was captivated by Josephine, both before and for some time after their marriage, seems clear. She was an older woman, rather fragile in health, and from a higher social class, and she was taken aback by his ardor and determination, and perhaps by his manners. She needed persuading, and he was not a persuader but a man of action, in personal as in public matters. She complained that, in bed, he was too quick and selfish. Later, she was swept along in the chariot of his success, as first lady of the Republic, then as empress, leading the life of palaces and the court. She spent a fortune on clothes, probably her chief interest in life. The couple were apart a great deal and, when together, were not close. The pair have been the victims of one of the most famous bedroom jokes of all time: "Not tonight, Josephine." There is no contemporary authority for it. What can it mean? It reflects, no doubt, what the French said. Josephine had had a number of affairs before she met Bonaparte. She seems to have taken lovers again during his long absences.

Bonaparte also had sexual encounters on campaign. As always with him, things were done in a hurry. When he felt the urge for sex, he would simply tell an aide: "Bring me a woman." They knew his tastes. These women were stripped and ushered into his quarters naked, Bonaparte having no wish to become another Holofernes, the biblical general executed by the ardent Israelite patriot Judith. Or rather, this was the belief of Bonaparte's nephew Napoleon III, who instituted the same practice when he, in turn, became emperor and needed a woman.

Both Bonaparte and Josephine were capable of jealousy. They had rows and shouting matches. Josephine could take risks because her position as spouse was protected by Bonaparte's superstition: he believed she was part of his destiny. Then why no child? She believed, on the advice of her doctor, that the deficiency lay in Bonaparte. After all, she had produced a son before. He believed that she would die before him, and that he could then remarry and produce offspring. He had women even when they were together in one of his palaces, as she was aware when she was denied entrance to his private quarters in the evening. (Perhaps this is the origin of the notorious joke.) But on neither side did the liaisons go deep. Bonaparte would joke about his own, sometimes to Josephine herself, criticizing the object of his interest, especially deficiencies in lovemaking. This was coarse, but Josephine doubtless took it as evidence that his affections were not deeply engaged. He evidently detested her own infidelities, but kept his deepest feelings to himself.

There was one important exception to Bonaparte's casual liaisons. Traveling triumphantly through Poland in the winter of 1806, he was serenaded by a group of wellborn girls, dressed as peasants, at one of the coach stops. He was struck by the beauty of one of them, and issued orders she was to be found and produced for him. She turned out to be the eighteen-year-old wife of the elderly count Walewski, mother of a little boy. She had no desire to become Bonaparte's mistress, but intense pressure was put on her by the Polish authorities, by her husband, and by her family to submit. She was told that Poland's independence would depend on her compliance. According to her own account, when she was finally pushed into Bonaparte's bedroom and rejected his embraces, he shouted at her: "If you enrage me, I will destroy Poland like this watch"—throwing his watch on the floor and stamping on it. She then fainted and, while she was unconscious, he raped her. In due course she warmed to him, left her husband, became pregnant, and gave birth to a son. Bonaparte was delighted. The event finally convinced him that he could produce an heir who would perpetuate his dynasty. Thus Josephine's days as empress were numbered and divorce was only a matter of time. But the countess Maria Walewska was not to be the beneficiary. She was ordered to return to her husband and register the child as his (in due course, Count Alexandre Walewski became foreign minister to Napoleon III). Bonaparte told his brother Lucien: "It would be my personal preference to give my mistress a crown. But reasons of state force me to ally myself with sovereigns."

Which sovereign now became the question. Bonaparte would have preferred to marry a Russian princess. Of all the legitimate sovereigns of Europe, Czar Alexander I was the only one Bonaparte liked, or said he did. He referred to him as "my friend." Friendship, which carried a special meaning for Bonaparte (it meant a pooling of interests as well as mutual affection), was the most important link he recognized, next to family. Marriage into Alexander's line would create a blood pact with the most powerful state in eastern Europe. There was everything to be said for the firmest possible links with Russia, not least the possibility of joint action in Asia to undermine Britain's Indian empire.

Alexander would not have it, though he avoided an open rejection of the plan. He was an ideologue, who held legitimacy to be sacred. His reasons were as much religious as dynastic. Bonaparte was the beneficiary of a godless revolution that had actively persecuted God's ministers on earth. True, he had made it up with the Roman church, but for transparent motives of expediency, and was quite capable of resuming the persecution if it once more became profitable. Again, if a Russian princess married Bonaparte, she would be forced to abjure Orthodoxy and embrace Catholicism. That might stir up the czar's Catholic subjects in Poland, with whose aspirations, in any case, Bonaparte had identified himself. The czar's refusal to sanctify his friendship with Bonaparte by a Christian family marriage was one of the most momentous mishaps in the dictator's career. Such an alliance would have made the eventual clash between France and Russia far less likely; might have ruled it out altogether, especially if the two powers began cooperating against Turkey and British India. In that case, Bonaparte might have remained arbiter of much of Europe indefinitely. As it was, however, the czar's refusal made the eventual invasion of Russia more likely, for Bonaparte deeply resented this rebuff from his "friend," and his subsequent analysis of the czar's acts and motives became far more hostile.

Where the Romanovs refused to mingle their blood with the Corsican adventurer's, the Habsburgs were perfectly willing, though it took them a little time to grow accustomed to the idea. For the Habsburgs, marriage was their geopolitics. They had, over the centuries, put together one of the largest empires in Europe, which had no common ethnic basis, entirely by marriage. They might not be very proficient at winning battles, but they were immensely shrewd and experienced in directing their sons toward land-rich heiresses and pairing off their daughters with powerful princes. Bonaparte might be a usurper, but he controlled half of Europe and terrified the rest. That was good enough for the family firm, and a bargain was struck.

Marie-Louise was not only the daughter of the Habsburg emperor; she was the great-niece of the murdered Marie-Antoinette. She had been brought up to regard the events of the 1790s in France as the most horrific catastrophe in the whole of European history. Perhaps they portended the coming of the Antichrist, and perhaps Bonaparte himself was indeed the Antichrist—that was her schoolroom teaching. Now she was told to marry the Ogre. Her ideological world was abruptly turned upside down. But the Habsburgs' training was strict. Their princesses expected to be married off to powerful men who might be objectionable in appearance, habits, morals, religion, or nationality. At least Bonaparte was comparatively young, professed the same faith, and exuded an excitement that could be felt all over Europe. So Marie-Louise went to her sacrificial fate in Paris with mixed feelings. Bonaparte took to her, or seemed to. She was big, blond, and sumptuous. She was also slow. Impatient as ever, he would hustle her along, slapping her broad rump and saying, "Get a move on!"

The marriage was celebrated on a prodigious scale. Good taste, or more likely Bonaparte's superstitious instincts, forbade a repetition of the sacrilegious, and in retrospect unlucky, coronation ceremony in Notre Dame. The 1810 wedding to Marie-Louise was a pronouncedly more secular affair and was held in the Louvre, the actual marriage rite being conducted in a gallery fitted up as a private chapel. Style, fashion, iconography had moved on in the last half-dozen years. In 1804 a colossal portrait-statue of Charlemagne had dominated the temporary porch of Notre Dame erected for the ceremony. Now, the décor was put into the skillful hands of Pierre-Paul Proud'hon, perhaps the greatest draftsman of the female nude France has ever produced, chosen because of his outstanding skills as a classicist. The theme was Roman, indeed Caesarian—the bounds of Bonaparte's empire had expanded from the Carolingian to projects that embraced all Europe and the Mediterranean. Huge triumphal arches were set up, façades transformed. The basic material, as usual in Revolutionary and Napoleonic fêtes, was cardboard. It was cheap, light, easy to set up and take down, and could be painted or covered in decorative materials with great effect. In retrospect, of course, it symbolized the ephemeral nature of the entire regime, but at the time it impressed as French chic and cleverness.

Bonaparte supervised all the details, down to the dress of his bride. One of the many things he thought he knew all about was women's fashions, and he often pronounced on the subject, in public, complimenting or disparaging ladies for their attire when they appeared at his state functions. For a woman to be assessed sartorially by the emperor was one of the many terrors of his court. He saw Marie-Louise as the product of a dowdy, provincial society—the term Biedermeier, as the verdict on all that was most frumpish in Viennese art, at this time had not yet come into use, but the sneering, especially among the French, had already begun—and he took it upon himself to dress her in the height of Parisian fashion, as he interpreted it, of course. But without the fashion-conscious Josephine at his side anymore, the results were not always felicitous. After the divorce, Josephine retired to her estate at Malmaison, dying in 1814.

The occasion itself had its uncomfortable, not to say brutal, moments. Although only 100 or so were invited to the actual wedding breakfast, some 8,000 notables—the entire Bonapartist *nomwenklatura,* one might say—had been summoned to the Louvre to line the galleries through which the wedding procession passed. In the Grande Galerie, the climax of the parade, the bride had to pass beneath stolen masterpieces by Leonardo da Vinci, Raphael, Rubens, and other masters, looted from Antwerp and Potsdam, Rome and Florence, Milan, Brussels, Munich, and, not least, Vienna, some of them having been prized items in her father's palaces. In a sense, she had been looted, too, or so many of those present must have felt.

The breakfast was an uneasy occasion. Bonaparte had noticed that the actual wedding ceremony, conducted not by the pope this time but by the Corsican uncle, Cardinal Fesch, had been boycotted by thirteen cardinals, who believed that the earlier marriage to Josephine had never been satisfactorily annulled and that therefore the new one was bigamous. He spent much of the meal fuming and thinking out a way of humiliating the disrespectful prelates—he eventually had them chased out of their official apartments and hustled literally into the street, red robes flapping.

The meal had its peculiarities in any case. Bonaparte was unsure whether to arrange the *placement* on the basis of precedence, or by alternate sexes, or according to the style of the ancien régime. In the end he hit upon the awkward arrangement of seating the men down one side of the table and the women on the other. Someone had put it into his head that he and his bride, as chief guests, ought to be honored by a *nef* apiece. These marvelous constructs of silver-gilt and jewelry, in the form of a ship, were the crowning feature of late-medieval and Renaissance table decorations. The two made for this occasion by the leading silversmith Henri August were of fitting splendor. But Bonaparte, like most people unfamiliar with the niceties of ancient ceremonial, thought they were merely decorative. Actually, they had a specific use: to hold the knives, forks, and spoons of the particular guest they honored, and his or her individual pots of condiment and spices, so no sharing with other guests was needed. Marie-Louise's father would have known this, but she was perhaps too young, and Bonaparte had no idea what they were for. So he had the *nefs* put on little tables by the side, for glory, and their whole point was lost.

What occurred on the wedding night is not recorded. But there is a story that Bonaparte, well aware that his ability to beget a son by this virgin bride was now at stake, and aware, too, that he was twice her age, put on one of his best sexual performances. But it was too quick, of course. The bride, thus bedded with the Ogre, was totally silent before the act and during it, and for some time afterward was lost in thought. Then she suddenly said, to the emperor's consternation: *"Do it again!"* At all events, then or later, a son was conceived, the future king of Rome. Proud'hon was again at hand to design the cradle: a sumptuous confection, chiefly in gold and enamel, and in the strictest Empire style, perhaps the most expensive *berceau* ever made in France. But it was of course an object of state, not of taste, as indeed were most of the artifacts created for the emperor's service.

Marie-Louise was said to have developed a strong personal attachment to the emperor, but it did not survive his absences and failure. In 1814 she set off from Vienna to join her husband in Elba, or so he ardently hoped. But whether by accident or design, her escorting gentleman was handsome and attentive, and she never got there. The Congress of Vienna made her reigning duchess of Parma, and she remarried twice, ending her days in 1847 in her father's old capital. The countess Walewska, on the whole, was more loyal to Bonaparte's memory. She visited him in Elba, perhaps believing that he was not finished yet and that her son might still be made king of Poland should Bonaparte's fortunes revive. But it was not to be, and she died, a disappointed woman, in 1817, aged only twenty-eight.

In any case, the birth of the king of Rome came too late for Bonaparte to adopt a long-term imperial policy. That would have involved him in a conscious and consistent effort to govern in the interests of the people he ruled. Of course, that is what he said he did anyway, and perhaps he half-believed it. He saw himself as the Enlightenment embodied, bringing rationality and justice to peoples hitherto ruled in the interests of privileged castes. But, despite the cheers that usually greeted him when he erupted into territories ruled by feudalism and autocracy, and some initial efforts to curry favor, Bonaparte was always forced in the end, and usually sooner rather than later, by financial and military necessity, to impose burdens that made his rule even more unpopular than the old regimes. His requirements for money and manpower were insatiable. The empire had to provide them, and hatred was the inevitable result. Moreover, if he overthrew one privileged caste, he replaced it with another, the French administration, civil and military. Most of Europe thus grew to hate him, collectively and individually, until these opponents swelled into a mighty multitude, excluding only those who benefited directly from his power.

One people who had a peculiar detestation of Bonaparte were the Swiss. His first act in Switzerland was to plunder the treasury in Berne: he took every gold and silver coin it contained to finance his expedition to Egypt. About £10 million in cash disappeared, plus £8 million in good paper, mainly English bills. When the French plenipotentiary, General Brune, left Switzerland for Italy, the bottom of his carriage collapsed under the weight of the stolen gold he had hidden in its luggage compartment. When the people resisted, they were shot. One French commander, General Schauenberg, slaughtered 500 men, women, and children in the Nidwalden; whole villages were wiped out. It was this rape of peaceful, liberty-loving Switzerland that decisively turned Wordsworth against Bonaparte. Wordsworth saw the Swiss as his realized ideal peasantry, loving their native land and close to it, yeomen who owned their own patches and worked them industriously, natural democrats whose ancient ways of governing themselves locally had been brutally smashed by a grasping and corrupt tyrant.

This was the pattern throughout occupied Europe. To the ordinary people, as opposed to the intellectuals of the towns, the coming of Bonaparte's armies often meant the loss of their crops, stores, horses, and livestock, the torching of their farms and barns, the rape of wives and daughters, the billeting of rapacious soldiery, and the stabling of horses in their beloved local church. Bonaparte's orders to commanders were: You have the force, live off the land. When in 1808 he put Marshal Joachim Murat in charge of conquered Spain, and the marshal complained to him of want of supplies, Bonaparte replied harshly that he was tired of a general who "at the head of 50,000 men, asks for things instead of taking them." The letter, said Murat, "stunned me like a tile falling on my head."

The Italians had mixed feelings about Bonaparte from the outset. On the one hand they welcomed this scourge of the occupying Austrians, this liberator. That made him popular in Lombardy. In the Papal States, the worst-governed part of Italy, he was seen as the man who, while protecting the church from revolutionary persecution, cut it down to size politically. Again, in Naples, Bonapartism was seen, initially, as preferable to the Bourbons. Bonaparte's brother-in-law, Murat, who had married the emperor's sister Caroline, was initially welcomed as substitute king. Few regretted, at the time, the suppression of knightly rule in Malta or the old self-perpetuating oligarchy that had ruled Venice.

Indeed, most of them saw him as an Italian. Bonaparte

himself boasted: "My origin has made all Italians regard me as a compatriot!" He said that when his sister Pauline proposed to marry a prince of the ancient Roman house of Borghese, the Italians said: "It will do, it's among ourselves, it's one of our own families." When Bonaparte ordered the pope to come to Paris to crown him as emperor, the Italian party among the cardinals overruled the Austrian party and encouraged him to accept. The argument went: "After all, we are imposing an Italian family on the barbarians, to govern them. We are revenging ourselves on the Gauls."

But this soon became a bad joke. The two Bonaparte princesses were themselves popular, Caroline for her charity to Naples's countless poor, Pauline for her entertaining naughtiness. Prettiest of all the women in the family, she was proud and shameless and loved to display her body. Once a week, she held *la cérémonie des pieds,* in which her exquisite little feet were washed and powdered by her maids, in front of a goggling circle of male aristocrats, and even the odd cardinal. She also forced Canova, Europe's leading sculptor, who was prudish, to portray her naked to the waist (he refused to do her totally naked, as she wished), lying on a bed. Inside the bed was a mechanism that moved the body around, so that it could be seen from all angles, and this was a candlelight after-dinner treat for Roman high society.

But French rule was corrupt and rapacious. The French stole any valuables not nailed down and many that were. The "barbarians" took hundreds of Italy's finest works of art, arguing that the Italians did not look after, know about, or care for them. Thanks to the efforts of Canova in 1815, aided by

Castlereagh and Wellington, many of these masterpieces, including the famous four antique horses of Venice, were returned to Italy, British troops holding back the whipped-up Paris mobs that tried to prevent repatriation. But more than a thousand precious objects dispersed in French provincial collections (a fact that undermined Bonaparte's claim that he brought the art of Europe to the Louvre so that the entire world could see it concentrated there) were never sent back and are still there. But money as well as art was stolen. Trieste, according to one eyewitness, was left bare. Other towns were effectively sacked. The various new states or republics that Bonaparte created in Italy were badly thought out and functioned even more inefficiently and exactingly than those they replaced. France taxed Italy mercilessly, and those who did not pay were treated as "brigands" and hanged. If villages or towns refused to hand them over, the mayor was hanged. Italy became a place where thousands of Frenchmen, usually from the families of marshals and generals, or others with influence, could get easy jobs as administrators, with large salaries and much to be made on the side. And wherever France ruled, there was cultural imperialism, or racism as we would say. Italian was treated as a barbarous patois. Thus, in Roncole, in the duchy of Parma, the baby Verdi was registered as *Joseph-Fortunin-François* by a grinning French official. When the débâcle came, most Italians found they preferred the Austrians, the papalists, even the Bourbons, to the hated French. Murat, who outstayed his welcome, was executed.

Most Britons never liked the look of Bonaparte from the start. William Pitt found by experience that his word could never be trusted, and Castlereagh and Canning in turn learned to treat him as an incorrigible liar. Even his faithful secretary Louis-Antoine Fauvelet de Bourrienne, one of his most favorable character witnesses, wrote: "It pained me to write official statements at his dictation, each one of which was an imposture." When he protested, Bonaparte answered: "My dear sir, you are an idiot, you understand nothing." But Bourrienne, and others, understood only too well. Bonaparte was a man who, when he was in his cradle, had been given by the Good Fairy gifts beyond the imagination of most men. But she had denied him things that most people, however humble, take for granted—the ability to distinguish between truth and falsehood, or right and wrong.

The British sensed this early on, especially Pitt and Castlereagh, both of whom prided themselves on never lying to the House of Commons. Lord Liverpool, who as a young man had actually witnessed the fall of the Bastille, and had never forgotten the horror of it, saw Bonaparte as the man who had turned a mob into an army to terrorize Europe. Ordinary British people, with their inherited hatred of standing armies and their passionate love of the navy, saw Bonaparte as an enormous standing army personified, and the navy as their heaven-sent protection from him. Everything Bonaparte did was wrong—or, if apparently benevolent, suspicious. Nelson himself summed up this intuitive rejection of Bonapartism. Picking up a pair of tongs, he said: "It matters not which way I place these tongs. But if Bonaparte says they must be placed *this way,* then we must place them the other."

The English intellectuals, if that is not too fancy a term,

were divided. With few exceptions, the artists were hostile, and rejected totally Bonaparte's notion that the arts of the world be concentrated in Paris in the Louvre—the fact that he renamed the building the Musée Napoléon was seen as insufferable impudence coming from a soldier. Many writers had been initially captivated by the Revolution. Wordsworth, who wrote "Bliss was it in that dawn to be alive, but to be young was very heaven," wanted to found a "pantisocracy" with Southey and Coleridge in America, to embody the new ideals. But all three turned against it, the brute facts of the Terror being more persuasive, perhaps, than the powerful arguments of Edmund Burke. But Burke carved the case against Revolutionary France (and by implication Bonaparte, its residual heir) in flaming tablets of stone. His hugely successful and much-read essay *Reflections on the Revolution in France* played a key role in keeping the thinking part of the nation steady during the long years of gloom-laden warfare that followed.

Wordsworth was particularly bitter about Bonaparte's cruelty to the peasants in the lands he invaded. Southey wrote his brilliant, bestselling *Life of Nelson*, which the entire nation read and which remained the standard work for a century. Coleridge learned a great deal about geopolitics (for which he had an instinct) while secretary to the governor of Malta during the buildup to the Trafalgar campaign in the Mediterranean, and he became a close friend of the British military expert Captain Charles William Pasley, whose book on British global strategy was so much relished by Jane Austen. Coleridge held Bonaparte in peculiar detestation. He wrote dozens of leading articles for the *Morning Chronicle* denouncing Bonaparte's policies and actions, which he argued were a threat to everything Britain stood for, from personal freedom to the independence of nations. Bonaparte was "the evil genius of the planet." He even thought there was a case for assassinating him. He saw him in colossal terms, not as a supernatural Antichrist so much as a superhuman monster, "the enemy of the human race," who was "waging war against mankind."

A few, Keats and Shelley among them, continued to recognize in Bonaparte the romantic hero, the man who broke into Egypt like a modern Alexander, or led his army across the Great Saint Bernard Pass like Hannibal. They fell in fact for the propaganda, turned into actual images of the man by Bonaparte's well-coached teams of portrait and history painters, Gros, David, and the rest. In the twentieth century, this infatuation was to occur time and again: George Bernard Shaw and Beatrice and Sidney Webb falling for the Stalin image, Norman Mailer and others hero-worshiping Fidel Castro, and an entire generation, including many Frenchmen such as Jean-Paul Sartre, praising the Mao Zedong regime, under which sixty million Chinese perished by famine or in the camps. Similarly, the cult of Bonaparte was originally wide, but it did not last. Those in England who clung to it did so more as a criticism of British institutions and ruling personalities than in approval of his doings. Thus Charles Lamb, who detested the prince regent, thought Bonaparte a "fine fellow" and said he would be happy to stand, cap in hand, at his table. Byron came to see that Bonaparte was a flawed hero, but regretted that he did not die at the head of his troops—the campaigns of 1813–14, he wrote, had "pared him away to gradual insignificance." It was a sad day when he was forced to "abdicate the throne of Europe." Bonaparte's one British admirer throughout all his crimes and vicissitudes was William Hazlitt. As an artist and critic, he had found Bonaparte's plan to gather the world's art in the Louvre, which he visited during the brief Peace of Amiens, an admirable project. But it was Hazlitt's hatred of "legitimacy," the capital sin of the ancien régime, that made him welcome Bonaparte as its enemy. He ignored Bonaparte's own assumption of the throne and attempts to secure legitimacy by his second marriage. Hazlitt regarded Waterloo as a total disaster: he was so cast down by it that he almost became a hopeless alcoholic, though he survived to write his ten-volume *Life of Napoleon,* most of it copied from secondary sources, which (I think) few have actually read through, from that day to this.

Many Americans, like the British, continued to sympathize with the Revolutionary aims of the regime, even though they hated the Terror. A few, like Thomas Jefferson, defended it, though in a halfhearted, half-ashamed manner, and when the regime returned to monarchy, France and its amazing despot were pigeonholed as just one more European autocracy. Jefferson never said another word of personal admiration for Bonaparte after he made himself emperor. He said Bonaparte's policy was "so crooked it eludes conjecture." British efforts to circumvent Bonaparte's Continental System, which banned the import or transit of British-owned or -manufactured goods, eventually drove the United States into war with the

British Empire, an unhappy conflict that damaged both sides about equally and was ended by a resigned acceptance of the status quo antebellum. Actually, most Americans were less impressed and affected by the war than by the astonishing offer Bonaparte made to sell America the whole of what was then called Louisiana, for what even at the time seemed a paltry sum of money.

The Louisiana Purchase must rate as Bonaparte's greatest single failure of imagination. "You have made a princely bargain," said Talleyrand to the Americans, not without a note of sadness. It was true. "Louisiana" comprised 828,000 square miles, subsequently becoming thirteen states. France was paid $15 million, or four cents an acre. If Bonaparte had used France's legitimate rights to its American territory to explore and create an enormous dominion across the Atlantic, instead of trying to carve out an illegitimate empire in Europe, he would have enriched France instead of impoverishing her, provided scope for countless adventurous young Frenchmen instead of killing them in futile battles, and incidentally inflicted more damage on his British opponents than all his efforts in Europe. He would also have changed the globe permanently, something his career failed to achieve in the end. But he knew nothing of America, and desired to know nothing until it was too late. He feared the Atlantic as a great ocean. He averted his eyes from the entire ship of the world to fasten them exclusively on its European cockpit, and thus in this respect betrayed his narrow, insular Corsican origins. So the United States was the power that permanently benefited most from the Bonapartist epoch.

The German intelligentsia, almost in its entirety, initially hailed Bonaparte as a hero. He was seen not only as the epitome of the romantic spirit of high adventure, in the eyes of the poets, but as the embodiment of the enlightened, all-powerful state, an ideal that appealed strongly to, among others, the young philosopher Hegel, whose exultation of the state opened the road to Bismarck's blood-and-iron Prussia and, still more disastrously, the Third Reich of Adolf Hitler. Hegel stood in the street, bareheaded, to see the triumphant Bonaparte pass, and sycophantically continued to applaud him even after French soldiers made off with his possessions. Later, as German opinion swung against Bonaparte, Hegel—who was anxious at all costs to be professor of philosophy at Berlin University—repudiated his support of French *civilisation*, embracing German *Kultur* instead. It could be said that he fell in love with Bonapartism for the wrong reasons, and out of it for the wrong reasons, too.

By contrast, there was Beethoven, working on his Third Symphony, the huge work that would break the mold of the old symphonic form forever. A friend and eyewitness, Ferdinand Ries, testified:

In this symphony, Beethoven had Bonaparte in his mind, but as he was when he was First Consul. Beethoven esteemed him greatly at the time [1804] and likened him to the great Roman consuls. I . . . saw a copy of the score lying on his table with the word "Bonaparte" at the extreme top of the title page, and at the extreme bottom "Luigi van Beethoven," but not another word. . . . I was the first to bring him the intelligence that Bonaparte had proclaimed himself emperor, whereupon he flew into a rage and cried out: "Is he then also nothing more than an ordinary human being? Now he too will trample on all the rights of men and indulge only his ambition. He will exalt himself above all the others and become a tyrant." Beethoven went to the table, took hold of the title page by the top, tore it in two and threw it on the floor.

Other famous German creators were more circumspect but equally dismissive. At the spectacular meeting of kings and princes at Erfurt in the autumn of 1808, Goethe, as Germany's leading writer and an important figure in the government of a small Rhineland state, was present. It was an imperial summit meeting, designed to impress. The palace, where the emperor took over, was transformed by a hundred wagonloads of French furniture, Savonnerie *tapisseries*, Aubusson carpets, Sèvres porcelain, gold and silver, a score of French chefs, and mountains of pâté, cheeses, hams, truffles, and cases of vintage Bordeaux and champagne. Except for the czar, the rulers all had to assemble in good time to greet the entrance of the emperor, when all stood up and bowed, and their ladies curtsied deep. The distinguished men present, from ruling dukes and cardinals to scribblers, waited for the imperial eye to fall on them. Bonaparte announced that Kassel was to be the new German capital. Johannes von Müller, the leading German historian, was to look after the details and write the emperor's life (as he had already done Frederick the Great's). Grimm was to be librarian and Beethoven the court musician. Other announcements would follow. (Little came of them.) Then

Bonaparte's glance fell on Goethe, who was summoned for an audience.

He found the emperor gobbling his breakfast, and stood watching him. He noted the green uniform of the Gardes Chasseurs, and Bonaparte's small feminine hand, hidden inside his waistcoat when not writing. Messengers arrived continually. Talleyrand came in with diplomatic news. General Pierre-Antoine Daru presented a report on the conscripted Prussian levies, now in training and eventually to be frozen and abandoned in the wastes of Russia. Goethe, despite himself, was impressed by the great man, now thirty-eight and getting plump, but ruling the world with a decisive phrase, a curt nod, a quick negative. Eventually he turned to Goethe, with an approving look: "*Voilà un homme,*" he said to his entourage. Flattery was quickly followed by the usual barrage of questions. How old are you? Have you children? What news of your duke? What are you writing? Have you seen the czar yet? You must describe this summit and dedicate your pamphlet to the czar, who will be pleased. Goethe: "I have never done anything of that kind." "Then you should start now. Remember Voltaire." Bonaparte smiled. "I have read *Werther* seven times. I took it with me to Egypt, to read under the Pyramids. It is part of the traveling library I keep in my coach. However, I have some criticisms to make." Goethe listened patiently. "Now, Monsieur Gött, let me come to the point. Come to Paris. I ask you most earnestly, as a personal favor to myself. There is a lack of great plays now. You must write them. Show how a great man, a modern Caesar, can bring general happiness to mankind. Do it in Paris and the

Comédie Française will present it with *éclat*. I implore you. I love the theatre. I would have made Corneille a prince." And so forth. Goethe listened courteously, bowing often. He made evasive replies. There was much comedy in this scene of the most powerful man in the world supplicating its greatest writer, and getting nowhere. Eventually, Bonaparte tired of his role and turned to a report on Poland. Goethe asked the chamberlain if he might be permitted to leave (he had stood for more than an hour). Bonaparte, without looking up, nodded. The last thing Goethe noticed was the strong smell of eau de cologne, which Bonaparte, as always, had sprayed lavishly over his body.

Bonaparte impressed different people differently, in his own age and ever since. There were natures to whom his busy, efficient, or at least continuous activity appealed, and those it revolted or made suspicious. There is a full-scale verbal portrait of Bonaparte at work, at his best, provided by Pierre-Louis Roederer, a journalist and admirer, a kind of official academic portrait corresponding to the painted ones of Ingres and Gros. It is worth quoting at length because much of it was true, much of the time:

> Punctual at every sitting [of the Council of State], prolonging the session five or six hours, discussing before or afterwards the subjects brought forward, always returning to two questions: "Is that *just?*" "Is that *useful?*" examining each question in itself under both relations . . . next consulting the best authorities . . . Never did the council adjourn without its members knowing more than the day before; if not

through knowledge derived from him, at least through the researches he obliged them to make. Never did the members of the Senate and the Corps Législatif, or of the tribunals, pay their respects to him without being rewarded for their homage by valuable instructions. He cannot be surrounded by public men without being the statesman, all forming for him a council of state. . . . What characterized him most of all was the force, flexibility and constancy of his attention. He can work eighteen hours at a stretch on one or on several subjects. I never saw him tired. I never found him lacking in inspiration, even when weary in body, nor when violently exercised, nor when angry.

Roederer wrote that this superman presided at meetings from 9 A.M. till 5 P.M. with a fifteen-minute break "and seems no more fatigued at the close of the session than when it began." Indeed, "his fellow-workmen break down and sink under the burden imposed on them and he supports without feeling the weight." Roederer quotes Bonaparte as saying:

Various subjects and affairs are stowed away in my brain as in a chest of drawers. When I want to take up any business, I shut one drawer and open another. None of them ever gets mixed, and never does this incommode me or fatigue me. If I feel sleepy, I shut all the drawers and go to sleep. . . . I am always at work. I meditate a great deal. If I seem always equal to the occasion, ready to face what comes, it is because I have thought the matter over a long time before undertaking it. I have anticipated whatever might happen. . . . I work all the time, at dinner and at the theater. I wake up at night in order to resume my work. I got up last night at 2 A.M. I stretched myself on my couch before the fire to examine the army reports sent to me by the Minister of War. I found twenty mistakes in them, and made notes which I have this morning sent to the minister, who is now engaged with his clerks in rectifying them. . . . There is nothing relating to warfare that I cannot make myself. If nobody knows how to make gunpowder, I do. I can construct gun-carriages. If cannons must be cast, I will see that it is done properly. If tactical details must be taught, I will teach them.

Bourienne wrote: "He had not a good memory for proper names, words and dates, but it was prodigious for *facts and localities.*" Another aide, General Daru, recorded that at his HQ on 13 August 1805, he dictated to him the entire campaign for the war against Austria that culminated in Austerlitz:

Order of marches, their duration, place of convergence or meeting of the columns, attacks in full force, the various movements and mistakes of the enemy, all this in rapid dictation, was foreseen beforehand and at a distance of 200 leagues. . . . The battlefield, the victories, and even the very days on which we were to enter Munich and Vienna were then announced and written down as it all turned out.

The modern reader can believe what he or she chooses of Bonaparte's boasting and the goggling admiration of his clerical staff and other witnesses. It may well be that he remembered the exact position of two cannons at Ostend at a time when the army had 6,000, or that he was able to give a lost platoon its exact line of march to rejoin its battalion in an army of 200,000—two typical anecdotes about his omniscience. But many of Bonaparte's prodigies of mental effort are no more plausible than the witticisms of royalty are funny. Those who served Bonaparte most slavishly had most need, for their own self-respect, to present him as a colossus. He liked to be surrounded by books and owned a great many at various times—even in straitened circumstances at Saint Helena, he had 3,370 books. But Madame de Remusat testified: "He is really ignorant, having read very little and always hastily." Stendhal claimed Bonaparte had not read Pierre Bayle's *Dictionary*, Montesquieu on the laws, or Adam Smith's *Wealth of Nations,* three works then regarded as indispensable for public men. He himself admitted he preferred to learn, through his ears, answers to the incessant questions he put. Unfortunately, keeping up a rapid fire of queries to impress his audience, he did not always listen to or retain the answers.

What is suggestive about descriptions of his work methods is his preoccupation with detail, which implies an inability to delegate. It was not unusual, in those days, for the man at the top to have to do it all. Wellington learned from bitter experience that there were few of his officers he could trust to do anything efficiently, or indeed at all. Necessity forced him to do all, at times. He grumbled that the British army, for instance, was centrally administered by only 150 clerks, whereas Bonaparte had between 8,000 and 12,000 at the French War Office—hard workers, too, who got in at 6 A.M. But from the accounts we have of Bonaparte at work, he appeared to reduplicate the efforts of these teeming, industrious bureaucrats.

The trouble with the Napoleonic Empire was that it had no natural or even artificial hierarchy. Immediately below Bonaparte, at the very top, were three key men (in addition to Berthier, the chief of staff up to 1814). Talleyrand ran diplomacy and much else. He came from a good family, but his nurse dropped him when he was tiny and he was permanently lamed. That meant he could not serve in the forces, so he was disinherited and put into the church, a career he hated. Made bishop of Autun early in 1789, he leapt at the chance offered by the summoning of the Estates General to join the Revolutionary forces, and thereafter served the new regime in all its many mutations, except during the Terror, when he emigrated to Britain, the United States, the Low Countries, and Germany. He served as foreign minister in 1797, promoted Bonaparte's interests, helped to organize the Brumaire coup in November 1799, and again served as foreign minister from December 1799 to 1807. He was everything Bonaparte was not: idle, taciturn, needing help with a dispatch or a letter, but immensely thoughtful and with a profound sense of what the nations of Europe were about, what they would stand and what they would not stand. Wellington once remarked of him: "He is not lively or pleasant in conversation, but now and then he comes out with a thing you remember all the rest of your life." Where Bonaparte thought in the short term, Talleyrand always thought in the long term, and this made him favor moderation. He wanted a durable peace from which France would emerge enlarged and strengthened, but not an object of intense envy and hatred among the other powers. He saw himself as a servant of Europe, in which France was only one historical unit, albeit the most important one. He helped to organize the various elements in Bonaparte's empire, especially the new kingdoms he set up. As Talleyrand took *douceurs* from all participants he became rich, though his profuse spending habits kept him always in need of more. But by 1807 he decided Bonaparte would never accept moderate counsels and was heading for ultimate ruin. Thereafter, while still in Bonaparte's service, Talleyrand established contacts with the Austrian and Russian courts and with other principalities, serving in effect as a double agent and collecting fees accordingly. Bonaparte knew about his corruption and double-dealing, in general terms anyway, and after the so-called Talleyrand-Fouché conspiracy, in which the emperor's two chief ministers were detected in a plan to replace Bonaparte by Murat, the emperor subjected Talleyrand to a lengthy and public dressing down in front of an astonished court. His parade-ground language was shocking, as in his tirade to Whitworth—he called Talleyrand "*merde en bas-de-soie*" (a shit in silk stockings)—and from that day to this, no one knows whether Bonaparte's loss of temper was deliberate or not. Talleyrand emerged the victor, saying nothing and merely bowing (as he had learned to do at Versailles when royalty was cross) but redoubling his contacts with other centers. The potentates learned to trust him, up to a point, and this was of invaluable service to France when Bonaparte's military power collapsed, for Talleyrand was the man they preferred to negotiate with. They followed his counsels of moderation, which the dictator had rejected, and so he saved France from a Carthaginian peace.

Joseph Fouché (1759–1820) was of coarser and baser material than Talleyrand but had the same capacity to survive. A spoiled priest, he became a Jacobin deputy, a Terrorist under Robespierre, survived the Thermidor coup, served the Directory as its Paris policeman, supported the Brumaire coup, and was rewarded with the job of chief of police to the Bonaparte regime, holding it until 1810. Fouché was not remotely loyal to anyone or anything, but he had a large staff, a big budget, and countless informants, and his *service de renseignement*, which covered all Europe as well as France but was particularly active in Paris, was of irreplaceable value to Bonaparte and helped to keep him ahead of the game and in power. He was never so secure after Fouché's removal in 1810. Fouché had decided the game was almost up and was systematizing his royalist contacts. This made him invaluable to France during the first débâcle of 1814, when he helped to restore Louis XVIII while remaining in contact with Bonaparte in Elba. Head of police again during the Hundred Days, he survived Waterloo and was once more in royal employment, when the outrage of the returned émigrés obliged the king to exile him. He died in Trieste in 1820, victim of such a ferocious bout of arthritis that it proved impossible to straighten his body and he was buried sitting up in his coffin. Fouché, who operated the world's first secret police force, and who was the prototype of Himmler or Beria, was an important element in Bonaparte's legacy of evil, for some of his methods were widely imitated in Austria and Prussia, where they became permanent, and even in harmless Sweden, where they were carried out there by Bonaparte's marshal Jean-Baptiste Bernadotte.

The third member of the trio was Vivant Denon (1747–1825), who became a key figure in Bonaparte's deliberate attempt to take the curse off his invidious reputation as a mere soldier and adventurer, and acquire a second persona as a cultural benefactor. Made head of all France's museums, at a time when the public collection was just coming into vogue, and art was beginning to be seen as something to be enjoyed by the middle class, indeed everyone, as opposed to an aristocratic elite, Denon could be seen as a progressive and an innovator. He can also be seen as a fig leaf on Bonaparte's naked dictatorship, a cultural factotum whereby the centralizing tyranny of the regime was translated into soothing artistic terms—the acceptable face of Bonapartism. He was a propagandist for culture, in the old clerical sense of the word, and his activities can be compared to the role played by Joseph Goebbels and Albert Speer under Hitler, or by André Malraux under President de Gaulle.

Bonaparte was by birth a quasi-Italian, but by national adoption he became a French cultural racist. He saw the appeal of French culture as a fifth column within the camps of his enemies, a force by means of which he could appeal over the heads of hostile courts to the intelligentsia, the young, the progressive, the bohemian, and the ardent throughout Europe. Hence Denon was at the center of a cultural web that reached all over the empire. Paris was embellished by the construction of the rue de Rivoli, its first modern thoroughfare.

Bonaparte did not have time to carry through his transformation of the medieval capital into a city of boulevards—that was left to his eventual successor Napoleon III. But vast sums of money were spent on sprucing up the city, now designated the world capital of civilization. The baggage trains of loot from the victorious armies, as they converged on Paris, loaded with antiquities as well as Old Masters, were labeled: "Greece ceded them, Rome lost them, their destiny has changed twice but it will not change again."

France's cultural manufactures, led by the magnificent royal porcelain factory at Sèvres, were revived and went into furious activity. Bonaparte characteristically appointed a scientist and inventor, Alexandre Brogniart, to run Sèvres, and many technical innovations were introduced. But the chief function of Sèvres, as of all other institutions, was to underpin the regime. There were many thousands of representations of Bonaparte himself, as general, First Consul, emperor; as busts, full lengths, or equestrian statues, nude or draped, with or without a crown, in porcelain or bronze, and in various sizes. There were countless busts, too, of both his wives and members of his family. Denon was instructed to oversee the creation of an exquisite porcelain hand of Pauline, made from a plaster cast, and of one of her pretty feet. Sèvres produced a magnificent Service des Maréchaux in 1810, in hand-painted porcelain, featuring Bonaparte himself and thirteen of his marshals, as well as sumptuous vases commemorating Bonaparte's victory at Austerlitz and his crossing of the Great Saint Bernard.

Denon and Bonaparte, indeed, restored and confirmed

France's reputation as the leading producer of luxury goods of every kind, from tapestry and furniture to women's clothes. Countless millions were spent on the refurbishment, from top to bottom, of France's great state palaces and houses, ministries and institutions—at any rate those Bonaparte thought worthy. The new rich of the regime, led by the millionaire marshals, followed suit, and the products of France's fashionable workshops were exported everywhere the French held sway. The style became known as Empire and was vaguely Roman, ornate, and heavily gilded. It was, indeed, an adumbration of the Gilded Age, when money was come by in vast quantities, none too scrupulously, and freely spent on grandeur. France was not yet even beginning to be industrialized, but its urban economy of skilled craftsmen flourished mightily under this patronage. That was an important part of Bonaparte's policy of keeping France as contented as he could, short of abandoning his ambition to rule all Europe. It was cultural imperialism and domestic stability as well. Significantly, the Ministry of the Interior had the following divisions: agriculture, commerce, subsistence, population, trade balance, factories, mines, foundries, religion, education, and an arts section involving theater, architecture, music, and literature. Its omnicompetence, so typical of Bonaparte's conviction that he, or the state, had the answer to everything, was the prototype of totalitarianism in its twentieth-century manifestations. Hence the reported saying of the emperor when told that France needed more good writers: "That is a matter for the Minister of the Interior."

The Denon touch was seen in the princely sums paid to

favored painters of the regime and its triumphs, such as Jacques-Louis David and Baron Gros. Handsome commissions were ordered to non-French artists of stature, too. Thus Canova did a marble statue of the emperor almost naked and more than ten feet high (he was used to these incongruous commissions, which included one of Washington dressed as a Roman senator). Scientific awards were made to non-French citizens, too, including the Englishman Sir Humphry Davy. (But such cash prizes were not always actually paid.) Under Denon's guidance, the French viceroy opened Milan's first public museum in 1805, Murat set up a museum in Naples the following year, and in 1809 King Joseph of Spain organized what became the Prado. There was a lot of rebuilding. In Venice, a palace fit for the emperor himself was started out of sections of the Procuratie Nuove and Vecchie, and much damage done, though happily the work was halted and reversed when Bonaparte fell. In Rome, in which Bonaparte had taken a particular interest since he made his infant son its king, he created the Piazza del Popolo. There were monumental schemes elsewhere in Europe, which remained for the most part visionary, like the grander projects of Mussolini and Albert Speer.

There was too much gilt in Denon's cultural presentation of the empire, and too much cardboard in his public shows. But on the whole it was the most successful aspect of Bonaparte's dictatorship, and one that served him well posthumously. For if Bonaparte had been merely a victorious soldier and conqueror, it would have been impossible in a country like France to have staged the public rehabilitation of the Napoleonic image that began in 1830 and continues to this day. Thanks to Denon, Bonaparte was able to play the cultural card with some success, and it still takes tricks.

Bonaparte's other strong suit was his reputation as a lawmaker, which allowed him to claim to be the Justinian of the modern world. The ancien régime had retained feudal and regional anomalies despite all the centralizing and modernizing efforts of Richelieu, Mazarin, Colbert, and the reforming liberals during the last days of Louis XV and throughout the reign of Louis XVI. The Revolution took up the cause, enacting nearly 15,000 statutes, then making half a dozen attempts to embody them in a homogenous code. Bonaparte, having absolute authority and a habit of taking rapid decisions, pushed the project forward. Despite his panegyricists, he attended in person only thirty-six out of the eighty-seven sessions of the Council of State needed to complete the draft code by the end of 1801. Its 2,281 articles were finally published in March 1804, when it was named the Code Civil and, from 1807 to 1814, the Code Napoléon. It abolished what remained of the feudal system and established, in theory anyway, the principle of equality before the law. It was imposed in those parts of Europe where the French writ ran, or rather where the French army occupied the barracks. The more rational and popular parts of it became permanent. Thus it had a huge impact on large parts of Europe, and it still has. Bonaparte did not create it. On the other hand it could not have come into being without him. Much of its apparent novelty was not new—after all, the English Parliament had abolished the feudal system in the early 1640s. Insofar as

Bonaparte's opinions were reflected in it, the code was conservative, or rather paternalist. It reversed the progress in
women's rights that had been made under the Revolution
(Bonaparte loathed women's interfering in politics, and his
view of their role was close to the *Kirche, Küche, Kinder* notion of Hitler). It enabled the French state to reimpose slavery
in the West Indies, at a time when Britain had just abolished
the slave trade by law. It contained many open or hidden pit-
falls for libertarians and weighted the balance heavily in favor
of public authority as opposed to the individual. It led to the
dark French saying about power: "Only *le Pouvoir* can cor-
rect the abuses of *le Pouvoir.*" But, with all its faults, it was his
monument.

The code gave the regime a kind of unity it did not otherwise possess. The Revolution had abolished the traditional
regional frontiers of France, which went back to the early
Middle Ages or even Roman times, and imposed *départements* and *préfets*. Bonaparte strengthened the new system,
using force and fear, but the old France was not so easily ex-
orcised. Even half a century after his death, perhaps a majority of French citizens did not speak what we would call
French. Bonaparte's dictatorship differed from its twentieth-
century successors fundamentally, in that it was not based on
a party. He had no party. Indeed, his regime rested on maintaining the balance among Jacobins, royalists, and other par-
ties. But if he had no party, he had an army. That was at
bottom—indeed on the surface, too—the source of his power,
and the army, though possessing the monopoly of force (even
over Fouché and his police), was not ubiquitous and perva-

sive in the way that a modern party is. Moreover, for its effectiveness as an instrument of rule, as distinct from war, it was naturally dependent on the men to whom Bonaparte gave authority over it: the male members of his family and his corps of marshals.

Neither group was suited to this role. Some were better than others. As monarch of the precariously artificial kingdom of Wesphalia, which Bonaparte knocked up out of Hesse-Cassel, Brunswick, and bits of Hanover and Saxony, his youngest brother, Jérôme, made a conscious effort to discharge an impossible job. The territory had a fixed income of thirty-four million francs, roughly. Ten million had to go to pay the French garrison (and in addition Jérôme had to raise an army), seven million went direct to the emperor, and a "debt" of fifty million a year went to the French state. So Jérôme had to live off capital by selling state property. There was no long-term future in this, and the kingdom would have disintegrated even if the Allies had not broken it up in 1813.

Eugène de Beauharnais, Bonaparte's stepson, who in 1805 was made viceroy of Italy (made up of French-occupied territories), likewise tried his best to govern well. Some of the Italians liked him, though they hated the French as a whole. He made a happy marriage, under his own steam as it were, to the daughter of the king of Bavaria, and there was an outside chance that he would survive the Bonapartist disaster of 1812–14 and keep his kingdom. Instead, the Congress of Vienna gave him a pension and made him prince of Eichstadt.

One of the most implausible of the new states was the Batavian Republic, which encompassed the old Dutch territories of the House of Orange, created by the Directory in 1795. Bonaparte turned it into the kingdom of Holland and made his brother Lucien its sovereign in 1806. These puppet kings had a miserable choice: to obey Bonaparte and risk total unpopularity among their subjects, or to disobey him and risk removal. Lucien chose the second course and was forced to abdicate in 1810, the territory then being absorbed into France. Brother Joseph, the eldest but most obedient of the siblings, took the other course, both as king of Naples and then, from 1808, as king of Spain. As a result, he was discounted as a cipher and proved an abject failure in both kingdoms. In Naples, he was succeeded by Joachim Murat, the son of a poor Gascon innkeeper, raised to a monarch by virtue of his marriage to Bonaparte's sister Caroline. Murat loved sensational uniforms and titles. He was, among other things, grand admiral of France, grand duke of Berg and Cleves, a prince of the empire, and a founding member of the marshalate, spreading across his broad chest a scintillating display of clanking medals and stars. He had some of the swagger Neapolitans love. But as Bonaparte's best cavalry commander, he was away a good deal in Russia and elsewhere, and much of the ruling was left to Caroline, who, though selfish and treacherous, was better at it. Left to herself, she might have survived the débâcle, but Murat, who had fled in March 1815, foolishly returned and was executed. She lived out her days in Florence as countess of Lipona, an anagram of Napoli.

Of the top tier of the Bonapartist state, the only potentate who survived the débâcle with his possessions intact was Jean-Baptiste Bernadotte (1763–1844). He rose fast to the marshalate by virtue of his marriage to Désirée Clary, a former Bonaparte mistress, which made him "family." In 1810 the obsequious Swedish states general elected Bernadotte heir to the childless Charles XII, hoping thereby to win Bonaparte's amity. The marshal, who had never won Bonaparte's approval as a commander (he was slow and cautious), thereupon switched sides and led Sweden back into the Allied camp. He proved a more effective king than general and kept his throne until his death in 1844, in his eighties.

Of course, Sweden was a real kingdom and a natural ethnic entity. So in a sense was the Grand Duchy of Warsaw, an ephemeral affair that Bonaparte created in 1807 and that survived as a French puppet until occupied by Russian troops after the retreat from Moscow. Spain and Holland, too, were mere usurpations, which naturally returned to the local lines when French bayonets withdrew. The other "kingdoms" of Italy and Germany were gimcrack creations, merely cartographical entities, put together by Bonaparte in one of his map sessions, and liable to constant changes of laws, frontiers, rulers, and constitutions. They played their historical part by removing ancient entities such as the Holy Roman Empire and crumbling states like Venice, and so accelerated the development of German and Italian nationalism and unity. But few, even at the time, can have believed they would survive. All of the puppet states and kingdoms were mere devices whereby Bonaparte could raise money and troops to keep his war going. At the same time, France itself expanded, in a cartographical sense, until it doubled its size and population, encompassing 130 *départements* in which 44 million lived. But this enlarged France merely increased the problems of governing it.

Bonaparte learned the hard way that military rule, or rule by military men, works only (if at all) in emergencies for brief periods. In a sense, then, the whole Napoleonic Empire was an emergency entity, built to blaze but not to last. The senior generals formed its integument, and in 1804 Bonaparte raised eighteen of them to the rank of marshal. The marshalate formed a college of military power and glory, to which would be added, from time to time, other distinguished generals, seven in all. The marshalate was not a threat to Bonaparte, for it had no corporate power or function and never met except socially. It was a convenient way of keeping his soldiers happy with the regime, especially since it was accompanied by titles and cash. Bonaparte was a patriarch, true to his Corsican origins, and treated his favored men-at-arms as a family of valor, to reinforce his family of blood. Some, like Murat, were raised to princedoms. Most became dukes. Thus Andoche Junot was made duke of Abrantes; Géraud Duroc, a mere general but charged with running the imperial household, was duke of Frioul; Auguste Marmont was duke of Ragusa; and so on. Most were given suitable estates, in some cases large ones, augmented by foreign properties. Bonaparte might also give a favored commander a house in Paris. He gave them incomes of 100,000, even 200,000 francs a year and presents of similar sums when they got married, and he was generous to their children. Bonaparte created an atmosphere of sumptuous luxury in his palaces and state institutions and encouraged the marshals to do the same, but was himself a man of parsimonious habits. He lived vicariously through his marshals (and other indulged servants and friends), keeping an account of his gifts in a notebook.

The marshals were a curious collection of old soldiers, romantics, daredevils and plain devils, time-servers and cynics. Almost without exception, they were brave men. The Gascons—Joachim Murat, Michel Ney, Jean Lannes, Nicolas Jean de Dieu Soult—were exceptionally so. Bonaparte called Ney "the bravest of the brave," and anyone who cares to see why should seek out his statue near the rue de l'Observateur in Paris, on which are listed the endless battles where he served with honor. Some had fought under the ancien régime, like the cavalryman Nicolas-Charles Oudinot, who carried the marks of twenty-two wounds he received under his new masters. About half the men had come up through the ranks. François-Joseph Lefebvre had been a sergeant in Louis XVI's guard and went on to lead the imperial guard infantry in Russia. Asked to justify Bonaparte's generosity to his marshals, the much-wounded veteran replied: "We will go down into my garden. I shall fire at you sixty times and, if you are still alive at the end, everything I have shall be yours." Some, like André Masséna, were incorrigibly corrupt, looters notorious even by the standards of Bonaparte's army. Masséna, indeed, was so outrageous that on one or two occasions he had actually to be punished by loss of command. But he was too invaluable to be kept in retirement, and he went on to become a marshal, duke of Rivoli, and a prince. Some were simple soldiers. Some, like Soult, were crafty survivors, who long outlived their master and flashed their stars at the courts of the last Bourbons and Louis-Philippe.

What few possessed—and therein lay their weakness—was independence of mind. They were, almost without exception, subordinates. Under the command of a decisive military genius like Bonaparte, they could perform prodigies. They rushed to obey his orders, to please him, to earn his praise and rewards. Sometimes, given an independent command, they acted well, especially if his orders were explicit and the task reasonably simple. But on their own, they tended to be nervous, looking over their shoulders, unresourceful in facing new problems he had not taught them how to solve. This exasperated the emperor, especially in Spain, where they all failed. But it was his own fault. He did not like to delegate, and therefore the men he promoted under his command tended to be those who carried out his orders with precision, rather than men with their own minds. The weakness was central to the failure of the empire, for Bonaparte used his marshals and generals not only to command distant armies, which he could not supervise in detail, but to govern provinces and kingdoms, run embassies, put down rebellions, and deal with all the crises that, from time to time, swept across territories of nearly eighty million souls.

There was something solitary and monolithic about Bonaparte. He was not the capstone of a solid pyramid of power. A huge unbridgeable chasm yawned between his person and the next man down the chain of command. And this fact, quite apart from the hidden menace of his personality, inspired fear. The state, the empire, was glued together by a ubiquitous terror. It was not that Bonaparte murdered many people. He imprisoned at will, and exiled. His police were everywhere and were very persistent. He controlled the printing presses, the theaters. His representative institutions were shams. But he had no concentration camps. His judicial murder of the duc d'Enghien—of which Talleyrand cynically remarked: "It was more than a crime, it was a mistake"—was remembered and brought up against Bonaparte again and again precisely because it was so unusual. But then it, too, helped to inspire fear, especially among Europe's princes and crowned heads, who felt that, if their armies failed them, they, too, might be dragged before the drumheads and sentenced to be shot.

The best account of the fear Bonaparte inspired was provided by Madame de Staël, whose book *Ten Years' Exile* is an indispensable guide to the Napoleonic period and a deep insight into the work of the man (not his mind, for that was unfathomable). De Staël was not a woman easily cowed. She was the strident daughter of Jacques Necker, the millionaire banker who had tried so hard to put into order the chaotic finances of the ancien régime. Rich and independent, articulate and outspoken, she had the unique distinction of being linked in possible marriage not only to Bonaparte himself but to his mortal enemy William Pitt. Neither intended any such thing; they rather fancied having careers of their own. So Germaine de Staël was no faintheart. Quite early in the Bonaparte dictatorship, she asked his aide Pierre Augereau if General Bonaparte intended to make himself king of Italy and was told: *"Non, assurément, c'est un jeune homme trop bien elévé pour cela."* De Staël found the remark curious:

> Far from reassuring me, further acquaintances with Bonaparte made him seem even more frightening. I had the disturbing feeling that no emotion of the heart could ever reach him. He regards a human being like a fact or a thing, never as an equal person like himself. He neither hates nor loves. . . . The force of his will resides in the imperturbable calculations of his egotism. He is a chess-master whose opponents happen to be the rest of humanity. . . . Neither pity nor attraction, nor religion nor attachment would ever divert him from his ends. . . . I felt in his soul cold steel, I felt in his mind a deep irony against which nothing great or good, even his own destiny, was proof; for he despised the nation which he intended to govern, and no spark of enthusiasm was mingled with his desire to astound the human race.

It is true that, at bottom, Bonaparte despised the French, or perhaps it would be more exact to say the Parisians, the heart of the "political nation." He thought of them, on the basis of his experience during the various phases of the Revolution, as essentially frivolous. And since Paris set the trend for the nation, the rest of France followed suit in

Paris's whims. He told a friend of Madame de Staël: "Something new must be done every three months, to captivate the imagination of the French nation—with them, whoever stands still is ruined." Thus, according to Wellington (who swore that the story was true), he sought to distract attention from his catastrophe in Russia by ordering the high-kicking dancers at the Opéra to stop wearing drawers—but the girls flatly refused. He thought the French clever and cunning but lightweight. They could not be trusted with democracy, or even with a parliament like the British one. The flattery he daily received confirmed this impression. De Staël relates that one of the state counselors, a member of the institute and a very great personage at Bonaparte's court, asked her: "Haven't you noticed what beautiful fingernails the First Consul has?" Another grandee asserted: "Bonaparte's hand is perfectly made," whereupon a young sprig of the old nobility interjected: "For Heaven's sake, let's not talk politics."

If Bonaparte despised the French, how much more complete was the contempt of this cultural racist for the rest of his empire. He turned their kings and reigning dukes out of their own palaces and slept in their royal beds. He dragooned their soldiers into his armies, where they became military helots. His system of taxation was deliberately punitive, for it kept them weak, as he believed, and it was the only way the empire could be saved from bankruptcy, which always threatened. Bonaparte believed that his foreign subjects would never rise against him, for he was the victim of his own propaganda.

What he did not grasp, because he did not listen to his critics, was that in trying to conquer all Europe, he was stirring up precisely the popular nationalism that had made Revolutionary France so formidable in the first place, but that was now spreading throughout the Continent.

What he did not grasp, and would not listen to his critics,
was that in trying to conquer all Europe, he was stirring up
precisely the passions and nationalist feelings the Revolution
set France so formidable in the first place, but that was now
spreading throughout the Continent.

CHAPTER FIVE

The Graveyards of Europe

THE DOWNFALL of Bonaparte had its origins in the unwill-
ingness of the British to accept his conquests and legitimize
them by a general peace treaty. After Trafalgar they were confident they could survive and somehow or other—they knew
not exactly how—checkmate his schemes. The Industrial
Revolution, based on steam and cotton, was proceeding vig-
orously, gold was flowing into the country, and the British
were confident they could both pay for an enormous navy and
also subsidize any or all of the powers willing to stand up to
the tyrant. Meanwhile, their navy kept station off the main
ports of the empire, twenty-four hours a day, 365 days a year,
keeping France's navies rotting in harbor, and preventing the
arrival or departure of any merchantmen carrying goods the
British ruled contraband.

This blockade had an effect on Bonaparte disproportion-
ate to its economic importance, considerable though that
was. He thought it was unfair, even morally outrageous. Un-
accustomed though he might be to discuss war-making in
terms of ethics, he nevertheless felt it inadmissible to use the
blockade weapon. Not understanding sea warfare, and under-
estimating the physical and financial strain of maintaining total blockade on vast stretches of coastline, he thought the

British were using this unlawful weapon on the cheap. As he later put it angrily: "With two small wooden machines, you distress an entire line of coast, and place a country in a situation of a body covered with oil, and thus deprived of its natural perspiration."

The issue was one of those occasions when Bonaparte allowed his anger to overrule his reason in determining the central strategy of the war. The idea of hitting back at British seapower and crippling its commerce by a universal blockade of British goods had been discussed under the Directory and the Consulate, but it was not until the end of 1806 that Bonaparte, flushed with his sensational triumphs over Austria, Russia, and Prussia in 1805-6, decided on action. On 21 November 1806 he laid down in Berlin a series of decrees aimed at excluding British goods and services wherever French arms held sway or influence. These were formalized in the first and second Milan Decrees (November–December 1807) and became known as the Continental System.

Bonaparte often passed laws or issued proclamations that proved ineffective, and nothing more was heard of them. But he took the Continental System with unusual earnestness and spent prodigious amounts of his time and energy trying to make it work. In vain. The system was counterproductive. It produced a vast amount of smuggling from which the British benefited, knowing full well that without strict maritime controls large-scale smuggling could not be prevented—and in this case the controlling maritime power, maintaining a perpetual inshore watch, was on the side of contraband. Moreover, inland efforts by Bonaparte's army and police to control the traffic were expensive in manpower and highly unpopular. This was true even in France, not least because the smugglers who brought in cheap British cotton goods and exotic products from the Americas and the East took back with them French wine, brandy, and silks for smuggling into Britain. But at least in France, some, perhaps most, people saw the point of the system. Outside France it seemed, to those who suffered the worst side of French imperialism, designed as much to boost French exports as to ruin Britain's. This impression was reinforced after Bonaparte issued the Trianon Decrees in 1810, which admitted some British goods under a complex tariff system discriminating shamelessly in favor of French producers. The result was that governments not directly controlled by the French, although part of the system, made little or no effort to enforce it. This was something Bonaparte's pride could not tolerate, and it tipped him into two disastrous wars, the first with Spain, the second with Russia.

Bonaparte had never fought in either of these two remote theaters, at both ends of Europe. Spain was a weak power that had come under French influence from 1796, lending its navy, allowing French troops to trample across the country to attack Britain's ally Portugal, and subscribing to the Continental System. Bonaparte despised the Spanish ruling elite, its armed forces, and everything else in a wretched country that had once been great and was now decadent and cowardly. He equally formed a low opinion of Russia, whose army he had scattered without much difficulty in the Austerlitz campaign. Lacking experience of Spain and Russia, Bonaparte was let down by what, as a rule, was his strongest gift or instinct, his geographical imagination. A man who could conjure up entire campaigns, down to the smallest topographical detail, by poring over maps embarked not once but twice on a desperate adventure cartographically blind. The maps, such as they were, did not convey, or did not convey to Bonaparte, the hazards and seriousness of these enterprises. Bonaparte was used to Europe proper, with its productive agriculture, teeming trade routes, good roads, prosperous cities, rivers bridged every few miles, and (on the whole) temperate climate. He knew how to squeeze it to produce what he wanted—he used it to supply his armies day by day with everything he required: food for his men and horses, money for the payroll, supplies of all kinds—and he knew, also, how to strike quickly at its centers of power, to compel surrender.

By contrast, Spain was, in certain important physical respects—climate, topography, vegetation and flora, desiccation, and soil content—part not of Europe but of northwest Africa. And in similar ways, Russia was part of northern and western Asia. Both had untamed, often unbridged rivers, poor or nonexistent roads, subsistence economies that could not support unsupplied armies, and extremes of climate that made both summers and winters perilous for troops without barracks. Neither country had a political core that, once occupied, placed the rest at the invader's feet. They were both eaters of armies.

Bonaparte believed that in Spain, a backward country in his eyes, he could build up a progressive pro-French party, as he had once done in Italy and Germany. But that did not work. Instead, the defeats and miseries engendered by the

French alliance, which exacerbated the decay of Spain's Latin American empire, its chief source of wealth, led to vicious internal disputes and the threat of civil war. Both factions appealed to Bonaparte to mediate. He took this as justification for ordering an open invasion, which took place in March 1808. He had no difficulty in taking Madrid, but when he then deposed the Bourbons and set up a puppet regime under his brother Joseph, switched from the throne of Naples at a moment's notice to take the crown once held by Charles V and Philip II, Spain's pride and dignity were outraged. In May there was something akin to a national uprising, which began in Madrid and spread rapidly after Joseph was crowned in June. A Cortes, or parliament, was elected under a national junta or government, and local juntas sprang up in most parts of the country. Joseph was king of Spain only in those parts where the French had a strong military presence, and if Spain was to be effectively subdued, a large occupying army would be permanently required.

Bonaparte had never confronted a situation like this. Austria, as he saw it, played the game: once it had been beaten in the field and its capital occupied, it sued for peace. The Prussians had done likewise after Friedland. Large garrisons, in almost impregnable and well-provisioned fortresses, had tamely surrendered when a mere troop of French cavalry had made its appearance. But in Spain the more troops the emperor poured in, the more resistance stiffened. There were 30,000 in Madrid, under Murat, appointed military governor. There was an army of 25,000 under Junot in Portugal, and another 20,000 along the Tagus, 15,000 in Catalonia, and

30,000 in reserve in Castile—120,000 in all. The Spanish army was beaten again and again, with no perceptible change in the overall situation. Soon there was no food for the French army and no supplies. All had to be sent from France, and Bonaparte refused to send it. So began the long, harrowing process of gouging food out of hoarding peasants, hanging and torturing them, and raping their wives, followed by the inevitable reprisals on isolated groups of French soldiers caught unawares, who were emasculated and burned alive. Spaniards who held office under the French were assassinated. Entire villages were torched in retaliation. Spain became a theater where all the worst horrors of war, so startlingly drawn and etched by Goya, were enacted.

Bonaparte took a personal hand in the last months of 1808. He brought with him more of his best generals, Soult and Ney, Lefebvre and Victor, and yet more troops. Joseph had felt obliged to evacuate Madrid. Bonaparte, with 45,000 men, had no difficulty in retaking it early in December. He immediately issued a succession of decrees and reforms, which fell on stony ground. He had an overall plan, which produced some minor victories and forced the withdrawal at Corunna of a 30,000-strong British force under General Sir John Moore, which had come to aid the junta. By January 1809 Bonaparte had been there three months and had had enough of Spain. He announced that he had solved the problem and returned to more congenial business in his empire.

But nothing had been solved. Though Moore was killed, his force was intact. Commanding the seas, the British found it relatively easy to embark a hard-pressed army and land it elsewhere on the coast. Moore was succeeded by Sir Arthur Wellesley (later Wellington). He had made his name in India and was therefore dismissed by his colleagues and the French as a "Sepoy general." In fact he was admirably suited to his task. He fought a war of attrition, designed to exhaust the enemy. He bolstered the Spanish forces and conserved his own. He had no hesitation in abandoning towns and territory when advisable and retiring behind prepared lines. He was a defensive general. But, when the odds were in his favor, he was quite capable of carrying out a well-prepared attack. Unlike Bonaparte, he had no grandiose strategy, no talent for blitzkrieg. He was a monument of patience, content with accumulating small gains. He recognized that the war for the peninsula was going to be a long haul, and he was right: it lasted for six years and was the most protracted campaign of the entire period.

In October 1809 Bonaparte sent 80,000 more troops to Spain, bringing the grand total to more than a quarter of a million. He put Masséna in overall command. Throughout the winter of 1809, for the whole of 1810, and into 1811, Masséna's strategy, an echo of Bonaparte's, was to bring Wellington's force to battle and destroy it. But Wellington feinted, dodged, and retired, and occasionally inflicted a sharp rebuff on the French. His troops were well fed and supplied, and Masséna's often near starving. Bonaparte was committing the elementary error that young cadets are taught at training school to avoid: "Never reinforce failure." The occupation of Spain was a failure. It either had to be replaced by an entirely different concept or abandoned. Instead, Bonaparte continued to send in reinforcements, small and large but never of a scale likely to make a dramatic difference. It became, for him, like Vietnam for the Americans or Afghanistan for Soviet Russia. And gradually Wellington's army grew larger and better trained, and his Spanish auxiliaries a little more dependable, especially when stiffened by British troops on their flank. So the climate of fear Bonaparte radiated was dispelled. Wellington began to advance and win battles—first minor ones, then major ones. Bonaparte blamed his marshals. Virtually all of them were tried out in Spain, and all failed. But, though Bonaparte criticized, he did not produce a new master plan. Nor did he again go to Spain himself.

The failure to win a quick victory in Spain, or any decisive victory at all, was one of the many reasons that led Bonaparte to embark on a war against Russia. It says a lot for his still-ebullient self-confidence, or maybe for his belief in his destiny, that having failed at one uncongenial end of Europe, he was ready to risk a second front at the other end, which was even less hospitable to his methods. One reason was pride. Bonaparte regarded Czar Alexander as unfinished business. He had come to terms with him at Tilsit and addressed him as "friend," something he never called the Austrian emperor or the king of Prussia. But their relationship was too akin to equality for Bonaparte's taste. He would have preferred Alexander, his army destroyed and his crown askew, to have come to him humbly to sue for terms, as the other legitimate potentates had done. Moreover, though the czar had confirmed his alliance with France at Erfurt in 1808, he had (Bonaparte came to realize and resent) insulted and disparaged him by declining to take up an obvious hint that he wanted the czar's sister in marriage. Evidently, the czar did not regard Bonaparte as fit to become "family." Despite all his victories and kingdoms, he was still illegitimate in Romanov eyes. So the emperor had to take Marie-Louise as a *pis-aller*. It had worked out very well, as Bonaparte never ceased to observe, but the injury was still felt. Hell hath no fury like a wooing emperor scorned. Then again, the Grand Duchy of Warsaw, which Bonaparte had created out of Prussian Poland in 1807, was an important source of Franco-Russian tension. It was ruled nominally by the king of Saxony, one of Bonaparte's puppets, but in practice by French soldiers and Polish officials. Bonaparte had dangled in front of the Poles the prospect of an enlarged and restored Polish kingdom, possibly under Jérôme, that would include much Russian territory. This infuriated the Russians. It is a fact of geopolitical life that you cannot be allies of both the Poles and the Russians at the same time.

However, the single biggest source of discord was the Continental System. Though the czar was pledged to implement it, it was probably beyond his power to do so. In any event, it was against Russia's economic interests. The Baltic trade was of vital importance to her (insofar as anything was vital to the Russian economy), and it had already been severely disrupted by the struggles of Denmark, which was a reluctant French ally, with Norway, Sweden, and Britain—indeed Denmark's alliance with France eventually forced her to go bankrupt and repudiate her debts. The ruin of the Baltic economy was evident by 1811, and so the czar was deaf to Bonaparte's complaints that he was not enforcing the system.

By the beginning of 1812, therefore, Bonaparte was bent on war. He lacked good maps of Russia, but he was not wholly unaware of the risks he would be taking. When Murat and four French corps had moved into Poland in the late autumn of 1806, they had suffered heavy losses, not from action but from sickness and undernourishment, as they crossed the barren and often roadless wilderness of the eastern European plain. And whatever the conditions in Poland might be, they would certainly be worse in Russia. But Bonaparte, whose last major victory had been at Wagram in the summer of 1809, was badly in need of something spectacular to reassure the French public he was still a superman, to restore his sliding prestige in Europe, and to compensate for the expensive stalemate in Spain.

Bonaparte intended to make the subjugation of Russia, and its integration into his Continental System, not just a French campaign but a European one. He persuaded himself, or perhaps genuinely believed, that his reforms and code had benefited his allies and satellites, and that the empire ought to be defended and expanded not just by a French army but by a Continental one. So from January 1812 onward he mobilized a historic European army, from Germany and Italy, Poland and Hungary, Austria and Bavaria, the Netherlands and Switzerland. When Alexander refused to enforce the Continental System in full without a slice of the Grand Duchy of Warsaw, Bonaparte stormed at his ambassador: "Does not your master realize I have 800,000 troops?" He did not have that many, but he could get together 650,000. Nearly all the army commanders, and the key staff officers, were French, and one-third of the men.

By the fourth week in June, the immense host was ready to cross the Neva and so move into Russia proper, preceded by a tremendous barrage of propaganda. Bonaparte thought the numbers would impress. But numbers do not impress Russians—they have too many of them already: countless people (or "souls," as they call them), villages, rivers, kilometers, high and low temperatures, areas, depths and densities of forests, marshes, plains, wildernesses. Russia always plays the numbers game at the extreme. In practice, the size of Bonaparte's Grande Armée, deployed in a Russian theater, was its weakness. It strung out at between fifty and a hundred kilometers, an easy target. In his German campaigns, Bonaparte had fashioned a form of deployment on the march in which an entire corps constituted moving squares for offensive or defensive purposes. It was called the *bataillon carré*. But that was impossible in Russia. Moving rather like a slow arrow, the army took eight days to pass a given spot. The supporting services alone stretched over ten kilometers, with 35,000 wagons, spare horses, cattle for slaughter, officers' carriages, ambulance trains, camp followers, and vehicles for transporting back the loot. There were 950 guns and a five-kilometer train of ammunition wagons. Bonaparte's propaganda machine boasted that the supply train included more than thirty million liters of wine and brandy. Whether it did is a mystery: the liquor certainly disappeared quickly enough.

Bonaparte had never directed an army of this unwieldy

size. On paper it was a miracle of his logistic skills. On the ground it looked too big and scattered. The emperor's plan was to move rapidly between the two Russian armies, defeat one or both of them if he could, then press on to Moscow. He calculated that defeat in battle would bring the czar to the negotiating table and, if that failed, the loss of the ancient capital, Moscow, would leave him no alternative but to capitulate. But from first to last the czar did very little, leaving his two armies to blunder about. In his imagination, Bonaparte saw the invasion as an effort by the South to conquer the North, for he identified himself with the Mediterranean South, as opposed to the great plains of northern Europe. And he was disquieted by his scanty historical knowledge, which told him the North had usually conquered the South. But the image was faulty; it was really the West invading the East. The great plains of Russia, in summertime, were baking hot and almost waterless. So the huge army's first unexpected enemy was heat, along with thirst, bad water, and the diseases it engenders. By the end of the summer, the effective strength of the army had been halved, and it had begun its fatal policy of killing its horses. The march became a trudge. Huge quantities of supplies were dropped off at food depots. But the peasants, as in Spain, could not be bribed or forced into replenishing the rations of the advancing troops. Torture made no difference. They burned their crops and, when possible, picked off the Grand Armée's stragglers to roast.

Not until the end of the first week in September, after nearly twelve weeks' marching, did Bonaparte manage to fight the big battle he had planned for. The Russian commander

Kutuzov had more than 70,000 infantry, about 25,000 cavalry and Cossacks plus irregulars, and 600 guns. He took up a strongly fortified position at the village of Borodino, on the route to Moscow but still eighty miles southwest of the capital. Bonaparte moved forward from Smolensk with an attacking army of 160,000 and more than 550 guns, but by the time it was in position to fight, it was much smaller. When battle commenced on 5 September it was still broad summer, and Bonaparte, aware that his marshals feared the onset of winter, said to them: *"Messieurs, voilà le soleil d'Austerlitz."* He and they remembered how the sun had shone through the winter mists at the great battle when he had routed large Russian forces. But those Russians had been more than a thousand miles from their homes, in a strange foreign place fighting a war whose objects were a complete mystery to them. Now they were defending their homeland. The main action took place on 7 September and lasted from six A.M. to six in the evening. The Russians withdrew the next day at dawn, in good order. Technically it was a Bonaparte victory, but the losses on both sides were enormous: 40,000 Russians and perhaps as many as 50,000 on the French side. Bonaparte, unlike the Russians, could not easily make good his losses, still less his huge expenditure of ammunition for the artillery, which had blazed away virtually all day at the Russian redoubts.

After this costly encounter, the road to Moscow was open, and the Russians evacuated it. Bonaparte moved in on 14 September, and the next day the Russian governor, F. V. Rostopchin, ordered the houses, mostly of wood, to be torched.

About three-quarters of the city was destroyed, leaving the Kremlin, which the French looted. There was much hard liquor left behind but little food, so more valuable horses were slaughtered and roasted, amid gruesome scenes of drinking and pillage. Bonaparte, disgusted and increasingly nervous, waited for the czar to capitulate. But the czar, again, did nothing. A personal letter from Bonaparte and two French delegations with treaty instructions were likewise ignored or rebuffed. By mid-October Bonaparte realized that the heavy snow was imminent and that there was no way he could keep the route out of Moscow open through the winter. He felt he had no alternative but to fall back on Smolensk, possibly farther.

Bonaparte marched his men out of Moscow on 19 October. But by now he was down to 95,000 effectives and most of his horses were dead. The Russians were beginning to counterattack, with ever-increasing forces, and on 3 November they destroyed the rear guard under Louis-Nicolas Davout. Bonaparte, much shaken, reached Smolensk on 9 November, to find that most of the food in his depot there had been eaten by starving stragglers, of whom there were about 30,000. When he left the city three days later, he had little more than 40,000 troops under his command. The snow was falling, retreat was becoming a rout, virtually all the loot had to be abandoned, and the army now had to cross several broad rivers whose few bridges had been destroyed. Bonaparte managed to get his army across the Berezina by 29 November, losing 20,000 in the process, but a few days later he had had enough. On 5 December he told his commanders that he was off to Paris as quickly as possible, to secure the regime there. They accepted the decision stoically. Murat was left in command.

It should be said that the retreat from Moscow, though horrific and shameful by the standards Bonaparte had set—more than 20,000 wounded were deliberately left behind, and the prisoners of war taken by the Russians, few of whom ever saw their homes again, numbered in excess of 200,000—was never a complete shambles. The Russian peasants had their revenge in full measure. But the Russian armies were in no fit state themselves to see a gratuitous battle, and on the whole they left the winter cold to do its work. The rear guard of the Grande Armée retired across the Neman in good order on 14 December, Ney, its commander, ensuring very properly that he was the last to leave Russian soil (he and Bonaparte's stepson, Beauharnais, were the only senior officers who enhanced their reputations during the disaster). Two days later, the emperor's notorious twenty-ninth bulletin of the campaign appeared in the official *Moniteur* in Paris. Blaming all on the winter, which had come "unexpectedly early," the text admitted that "an atrocious catastrophe" had overtaken the Grande Armée.

Meanwhile, Bonaparte himself had been lucky to escape a patrol of guerrillas. He traveled in three horse-drawn sleighs, he occupying one with Louis Caulaincourt, head of the imperial household, a trusted man who had organized the murder of d'Enghien. The others carried his interpreter, his Mamluk bodyguard Rustam, and five servants and aides. They were in the sleigh five days and nearly froze to death in the minus-25-degree temperatures. Bonaparte kept himself warm by taking

Caulaincourt's furs and by incessant talking, rehearsing his excuses. All his tirades ended in a curse against the English: "But for them I would have been a man of peace." By the time he got to Warsaw and received Polish bigwigs, who were aghast at the disaster, he had his quip ready: "From the sublime to the ridiculous is only one step" (it was Voltaire who had actually coined the saying). He repeated this several times during a three-hour discourse. The sound of his own voice being received in deferential silence by obsequious dignitaries reassured him. He hurried on into Germany by sledge, then by *calèche* and coach. The party broke the axle of one vehicle, changed into another, stopping only one hour in twenty-four. As they halted briefly in one German town, Bonaparte asked the postmaster its name, was told "Bonn," and called out: "Give my respects to Monsieur Gött" (Goethe), then rattled on. After a journey in all of thirteen days, they reached the Tuileries Palace in Paris just before midnight on 18 December.

The next day Bonaparte was at his desk, working a fifteen-hour stretch, sending peremptory letters all over his empire. But the signs were ominous. On 25 December, Prussia withdrew from the French alliance. Soon, Prussian troops were fraternizing with the Russian army. One corps actually joined forces to threaten the French withdrawal from Germany. In March 1813, Prussia declared war on Bonaparte. The next ally to desert was the pope, who renounced his concordat with France. The news from Spain was worse and worse. Wellington now had an impressive army of experienced soldiers, he had got the Spanish army under his control, and the two together—plus the guerrillas—were threatening to turn the French out of Spain altogether and invade France itself. The French position in Italy was beginning to crumble, and Bonaparte did not trust Murat (now back in Naples), who he thought, rightly, would change sides to keep his kingdom. Worst of all from Bonaparte's point of view, his father-in-law, the emperor Francis, was behaving shiftily. He said he was standing by his French alliance, but he was rearming fast. What for? He claimed it was to enable him to mediate effectively between Prussia and France. But he refused to communicate directly with Bonaparte, saying all must go through his foreign minister, Metternich. This tall, blond Austrian womanizer (he had had a liaison with Bonaparte's sister Caroline) was anti-French and believed in the balance of power in Europe, like Talleyrand. By saying "Talk to Metternich," Francis was in effect advising "Sue for peace while you can still get reasonable terms."

But once he was back at work, with the snows of Russia a rapidly fading memory, Bonaparte's optimism flooded back. The day after he returned to Paris, he had begun assembling a new army, calling up young conscripts and plucking back key men and units from all over the remaining empire. In April 1813, he was in Leipzig, on his horse once more at the *tête d'armée* (his favorite phrase). He looked fat and paunchy and old, but confident, and he issued his orders with great panache. It became the fashion among the French to say, "Isn't he looking well!" At Lützen, he inflicted a sharp rebuff on Prussia's leading general, Gebhard Leberecht von Blücher, personally leading an attack by the Young Guard. He drove the Prussians back over the Elbe, and beat them again at

Bautzen, forcing them to retreat behind the Oder. Then he returned to Metternich, who met him on 26 June in the palace at Dresden, capital of France's satellite Saxony. The meeting lasted nine hours, and it was not of the kind Bonaparte relished. He had to listen as well as talk. Flushed with his victories, he found Metternich skeptical and obdurate. To keep Austria neutral, he was told, he would have to surrender not just Illyria, for which he was prepared, but Lombardy and much else. To get peace with Prussia, France would have to withdraw behind the Rhine, and so on. Bonaparte was furious and threw his hat into the corner of the room in his rage. Such terms were tantamount to dissolving the empire and throwing away his life's work. In fact what Metternich offered was an agreement that, in six months' time, Bonaparte would have been delighted to accept. But many men had to be turned into corpses before that point was reached. Metternich, shaken by the emperor's lack of realism, asked him if he really wanted peace—did not the lives of men matter to him? Bonaparte told him that, rather than accept such dishonorable terms, he would gladly sacrifice a million. Metternich replied: "Sire, you are a lost man." The interview ended.

What Metternich grasped, what Bonaparte did not yet realize, was that a historic change was taking place in the German-speaking world that altered the whole strategic pattern of Europe. Bonaparte, in his desire to give a reforming cover to his territorial expansionism, had smashed to pieces the old Holy Roman Empire to replace it (as he thought) by a French-dominated Carolingian one. The results were a classic demonstration of Karl Popper's law of unintended effect.

Destroying the Holy Roman Empire seemed, to Bonaparte, no more momentous than ending the Venetian oligarchy or replacing the Knights of Malta. It was just dumping a medieval relic in the dustbin of history. In fact, the Holy Roman Empire filled a role. It was a device for stressing the cultural unity of Germany while making it difficult to bring about its political and military unity. Prussia was the largest German power, but Austria, by virtue of its hereditary occupation of the German imperial throne, was its equal, and the natural protector of the smaller German states. There was thus balance and multiplicity. The more responsible German thinkers wanted to keep things as they were. They argued that the balance between Prussia and Austria, and the existence of other German cultural centers, was of great benefit to Europe in music and painting, education and philosophy, theology and literature. Culture was Germany's gift to Europe, not power. If, on the other hand, Germany was unified, it would be much more formidable than its neighbors and would inevitably seek to dominate the rest of Europe. That, when their arguments were brushed aside, was exactly what happened in the late nineteenth and early twentieth centuries.

Bonaparte played the detonating role in this process. After Austerlitz and Jena, and the tame surrender of the Prussian army, he had treated the Germans with contempt. He had set up French garrisons and puppet rulers, personally occupied their royal palaces when he felt like it, and made German kings, electors, and reigning dukes parade before him like lackeys. He conscripted their armies to provide expendable manpower for his schemes. His propagandists held sway in

German universities, presenting French culture, with its strong classicizing flavor and its Roman gilt, as the only acceptable form of artistic expression. His puppets imposed a Gallic censorship on their press and books.

The political and military reaction was slow in coming, but it was all the more powerful, when the Russian catastrophe brought it into the open, for being accompanied by a deep-rooted and overwhelmingly muscular cultural reaction. The explosion in German thought and literature at the end of the eighteenth century was a determining event in European history. Coleridge was one of the first to become aware of its importance, and brought the good news to England. He thought that the imposition of alien French culture would turn German creativity inward, with disastrous consequences, and that was one reason why he hated Bonaparte so much, saw him as an enemy of the creative human spirit. Madame de Staël also examined the new German phenomenon and was overwhelmed by its richness and profundity. She wrote a brilliant book about it, which Bonaparte would not allow to be published in France, but which was printed nonetheless and widely circulated, and so brought the good news to Paris.

The young Bonaparte had been seen as a romantic figure. But that was a superficial judgment on a slim young man who had done remarkable things. The mature Bonaparte, stout and imperious, with his much-vaunted cult of reason in all things, and his dogmatic taste for *le goût roman* and *le style empire,* exported everywhere his soldiers took their bayonets, was increasingly seen by the intelligentsia as an old-fashioned relic of a dusty classicism whose day was done, and as an implacable opponent of the dawning romanticism his tyranny had evoked. That was why Victor Hugo, a teenage prodigy, hated him. The new spirit, which enthralled the young, came from the North—that was why it first took root in England and Germany. It was medieval and Gothic; it was both Christian and pagan as opposed to rational, rooted in folklore and legend, in spirituality and the supernatural, in the laws of the Angles and Saxons rather than the Code Napoléon, in the dark, impenetrable forests with their wolves and bears, rather than the sunny South.

The German intellectuals, writers, and artists, imbued with this spirit, were the first to turn against Bonaparte. It was significant that the German artistic colony in Rome, second in size only to the French, became fiercely francophobe in the years 1805–15. German painters adopted an anti-Napoleonic iconography. For a decade, Bonaparte himself had poured millions into launching an iconography of his own. To give one instance, Bonaparte sought to efface the massacre at Jaffa by holding a competition among French artists to portray him in a more heroic light. The eventual result was Gros's riveting painting *Bonaparte among the Plague-Stricken at Jaffa,* showing the young general dauntlessly defying the risk of contagion by comforting his stricken soldiers and civilians. It was an immense success and became one of the lasting icon-narratives of the regime.

Now the Germans moved in precisely the opposite direction, by projecting Gothic, anticlassical, and anti-Bonapartist images on the popular consciousness. One of the most vehement of the Gothic painters was Caspar David Friedrich, who hated Bonaparte and whose symbolic crosses, arising out of the snow or mist, were ideograms of Germany's mystic and Christian awakening from Gallic rationalism. The German romantic artists both joined and illustrated the bands of *Jäger,* volunteer detachments of forest rangers who were recruited to attack the French army, like organized guerrillas. They wore green uniforms, and one of them was Colonel Friedrich von Brincken, who was killed in the struggle. He wears the green uniform in Friedrich's most famous painting, the *Rückenfigur* or *Wanderer above the Sea of Fog,* which commemorates his memory, showing him rising above the choking miasma of Bonapartist oppression.

We come here to an important historiographical point. It has been common among Bonaparte's biographers to attribute his eventual failures to age, lack of concentration, deterioration in his health, increasing weight, and tiredness, and to a progressive decline in his mental faculties. There is some truth in this. It is also true that the French army was in slow but irreversible decline, so many experienced junior officers and NCOs, who should have been training the new intakes, having been lost in Russia. More than 200,000 fine horses had been left there, too, and they could not be replaced either. From this point on, Bonaparte always complained that he did not have enough cavalry or that it was of poor quality.

These are material reasons for Bonaparte's declension. But there was a metaphysical reason, too, embracing the intellectual, cultural, and spiritual dimensions. He had once been "a man whose time had come." In the second half of the

1790s, Bonaparte was an embodiment, all over Europe, of the protest against the old legitimists, their inefficiency, privileges, obscurantism, and misuse of resources, above all the talents and genius of youth. Thus he prospered and conquered. By 1813, however, he was out of date. His time had gone. His compatriot and critic Chateaubriand, who embodied the new romanticism, had produced a book, *Le Génie du christianisme,* that had a huge effect on French and European opinion and that captured the new spirit of the times. A religious revival was under way, and that was something Bonaparte, a secular man if ever there was one, neither understood nor wanted. Wherever one turned in 1813—to the bestselling novels and poems of Sir Walter Scott, read all over the Continent; to the later symphonies of Beethoven, still raging at Bonaparte's betrayal of his ideal; and to the etchings of Goya, relished by everyone who had suffered under Bonaparte's troops—the zeitgeist was against the French emperor. He did not understand that all had changed. He continued to splutter out, in an unending stream, schemes for the improvement of humanity. But he was a superannuated man, and events were about to deposit him, alongside the doge of Venice, the grand master of Malta, and the Holy Roman Emperor, on history's smoldering rubbish dump.

Meanwhile, the law of unintended effect continued to operate. The war for Germany, which opened with two victories for Bonaparte in April, continued for six months, punctuated by pauses and one truce. Gradually Bonaparte built up his numerical strength in Germany or nearby to 450,000 men in his main army, with a further 220,000 within call. But he was permanently short of cavalry to turn a tactical advantage over his opponents into a rout, and much of his infantry was undertrained and incapable of performing complicated field maneuvers. By contrast, the Prussian army benefited from fundamental reforms instigated by the violently anti-Bonapartist staff general Gerhard Scharnhorst. Bonaparte killed this brilliant organizer at Lützen. But he was quickly replaced by the equally forceful Augustus Wilhelm Gneisenau, who as chief of staff helped to make Marshal Blücher into a highly successful battle commander and turned the Prussian army into the most formidable military machine in Europe, a title it held, on and off, until 1945.

One can say, indeed, that 1813 marked the point at which the military paramountcy of Europe, which France had held since the 1640s, began to shift toward Germany. In retrospect, it is obvious that Bonaparte should have made peace immediately after his two victories in April and May. He would probably have got better terms than Metternich offered. As it was, in the Sixth Coalition, which formed during the year, he faced a more formidable array of forces than ever before. He had always said that, leaving Britain aside, he could beat two of the big three (Prussia, Russia, and Austria) at any one time. If he faced three, the outcome was more doubtful. Now, when Austria declared war on him in August, he faced not only the big three but Sweden, while his former ally Bavaria changed sides and his most abject puppet, Saxony, was occupied by his enemies. Moreover he was now fighting, in effect, a united Germany, which was being swept by a wave of violent nationalism that made the Scharnhorst-

Gneisenau reforms far more effective, and inspired even the Austrians to fight as they had never fought before. In numbers, Bonaparte appeared at times to have the advantage. But in quality, for the first time, the advantage lay with his opponents. As Wellington later observed, Bonaparte lacked the temperament to fight a defensive battle, let alone a defensive campaign. Had he been able to do so, he might well have fought the Sixth Coalition to a peace of exhaustion, without a single one of its soldiers setting foot on French soil proper. As it was, he was still determined to follow his instincts and bring the entire war to colossal battle, ignoring the fact that his own losses could not be replaced, while the Allies were increasing their numerical strength all the time.

The outcome was the Battle of Leipzig, fought over three days, 16–19 October 1813. The number of troops involved was greater than in any of the pitched battles of the entire period 1792–1815. (Borodino was the next largest.) Bonaparte had 180,000 men around the city and was awaiting 20,000 more. The Austrians, Prussians, Russians, Swedes, and other entities had in the area about 350,000 troops, with more on the way. It was called "the battle of the nations," a somber phrase, signifying what Bonaparte was doing to Europe, precipitating a new form of warfare that involved not just professional armies but entire peoples—total war. More than half those engaged were conscripts. There was no element of dazzling maneuver or tactical surprise in this battle of attrition, and the environs of the city became killing fields in which the total casualties were not far short of 100,000. Bonaparte was forced to withdraw, leaving behind an additional 30,000 prisoners, plus—a new note, this—5,000 who fled to the opposing camp while the battle was still raging. He left behind, too, 100,000 men in French garrisons scattered all over Germany, and all were forced into unconditional surrender.

Thus the empire dissolved in military ruin, and Bonaparte now had to fight, for the first time, on French soil. It was then that French public opinion turned decisively against him. The French had applauded Bonaparte's conquests, not least the way in which he got them to pay for his empire by financial exactions and to man it by providing many of the troops. But those days were over, and the full cost of any continued fighting had to be carried by France herself, both in men and in money. In 1812 and 1813 Bonaparte had lost, in killed, wounded, prisoners, and simply disappeared, about one million men. About half were Frenchmen. Yet all had been in vain, as Germans and Russians were now pouring across the frontiers into France, often led by marauding squadrons of Cossacks. All looted, raped, and murdered, as the French had once looted, raped, and murdered in their homelands. Thus faced with the horrors of war, as the Germans, Italians, Russians, and Spanish—and others—had faced them, the French did not like what they saw, and quailed. Wellington had now broken out of Spain, skirted around the Pyrenees, and was well into France. Soult, his opponent, had more or less given up the struggle. Bordeaux capitulated without a shot. The French and their puppets in Switzerland put up no resistance to the Austrians. The British and their allies occupied Holland and pushed into Belgium. Germany was totally lost. Major French frontier fortresses surrendered or were abandoned. Royalists began to appear everywhere in France, and Talleyrand and those who thought like him were maneuvering to get the best terms they could.

Bonaparte's behavior, in the interval between Leipzig in October 1813 and his actual abdication in April 1814, makes little sense. He rejected Allied offers first of the 1799 frontiers, then of the 1792 old frontiers, both of which might have given him a real chance of surviving as a ruler. He then, in January, took the head of his army again. But it was not an army that gave him even an outside chance of beating the Allies in a major battle, the only way in which he could save himself. It never numbered more than 70,000 men at its height, and the Allied armies converging on Paris were in excess of half a million, with more to come if necessary. Bonaparte had successfully played the numbers game in war and raised the stakes, and now the odds turned against him with a vengeance. All he could do was to carry out his old strategy in miniature—lightning strikes against isolated sections of the Allied forces. This he did with considerable skill, and his 1814 campaign in the winter and early spring is often held up as a model of how to use inferior forces with effect. The so-called Six-Day campaign of 9–14 February inflicted 20,000 casualties on the Prussians and was followed by several more victorious skirmishes. But they were of no more strategic significance than the Nazi victory in the Ardennes at the end of 1944. They merely taught Blücher and the other commanders to be more cautious and allow their steady buildup of forces, and occupation of French territory, to take effect. Bonaparte won his last victory, over a detached Prussian division, on 13 March. Two weeks later, he gave up the campaign as hopeless and made for Paris. By now his commanders were surrendering and defecting, and by the end of the month it was impossible to defend the capital. The empress Marie-Louise; her son, the king of Rome; and Joseph, nominally in charge of the imperial government, left in a hurry. About 150,000 Allied troops entered the capital, and Talleyrand, as vice-chamberlain of the empire, formally proclaimed the dissolution of the empire, preparing the way for a royal restoration. Bonaparte made a last attempt to assemble an army at Fontainebleau, but his remaining marshals refused to follow him, and on 6 April he formally abdicated the thrones of France and Italy. He was offered a petty kingdom in Elba, and took it, sailing for the island aboard a British warship on 28 April. It was a sad and messy end to a great enterprise, and many felt, like Byron, that Bonaparte should have gone down fighting. He had raised French nationalism to a gigantic height, but in the process he had awakened other nationalist forces that, collectively, overwhelmed him and his country. The *apprenti sorcier* should have gone down with his failed magic. But Bonaparte still had illusions to entertain and his appetite for battle was undiminished. So a long, dying sigh was in store, for him and his admirers.

CHAPTER SIX

Elba and Waterloo

BONAPARTE ARRIVED in Elba on 4 May 1814, courtesy of the Royal Navy frigate HMS *Undaunted*. The Allies rejected his demand that the abdication was in favor of his son, the king of Rome. Instead, Louis XVIII, brother of the guillotined king, was restored to the throne of the Bourbons and arrived in Paris the same day Bonaparte arrived in Elba. The whole thing had been arranged by Talleyrand, now on excellent terms with Metternich; Karl Robert Nesselrode, the Russian minister; and the three sovereigns, especially the czar, who chose to stay in Talleyrand's house when he reached Paris. Bonaparte saw Talleyrand's actions as treason, but the old fox could reply that he put the interests of France before any other loyalty, unlike Bonaparte, who identified France's interests with his own. Certainly, Talleyrand's tact and cunning performed an immeasurable service to his country by ensuring that France immediately became one of the big five, along with Britain, Prussia, Austria, and Russia, in restoring order to Europe after the collapse of Bonapartism.

As a sop to his pride, Bonaparte was appointed de facto administrator of Elba, under Allied supervision. His official title was "Emperor and Ruler of Elba." That was a joke, of course: one detects Talleyrand's sly sense of humor. Bonaparte did not see the point. One of the things he did aboard the frigate was to design a new flag for his little territory. His declension from Europe to Elba was indeed his maxim of the sublime to the ridiculous turned into reality. From ruling half the continent and eighty million, he was now prince of an island 7 miles from the coast of Italy, 19 miles long, 7 wide, 140 square miles in area, and with a population said to be 100,000, but which at the end of the nineteenth century was accurately counted as a little over 25,000. It had been acquired in the sixteenth century by Cosimo I of Florence. He had built its capital, which he called Cosmopolis but had become known as Portoferraio, and Bonaparte did not have the heart to restore its splendid name, or the chutzpah to call it Napoleonopolis. But he had his main palace there, and his villa outside, and various other properties on the island. These included a former hermitage, high in the mountains, which went up to 3,440 feet. There, in due course, he entertained his Polish mistress, Maria Walewska, who came on a visit, bringing their little blond boy, Alexandre. She was more faithful to him than Marie-Louise, who not only declined to come to him but soon (by the stratagems of Metternich) acquired a lover, her aide-de-camp, General Count von Neipperg (rather like the prince regent's estranged wife, Caroline, and her majordomo). Bonaparte made no comment on this. But when, soon after his arrival in Elba, he got the news of Josephine's death, he commented: "Now she is happy." He was delighted to welcome his mother, Letizia, now in her mid-sixties, whose attitude to the débâcle was "I told you so!" She had always treated his splendor as fairy gold and remarked: "Yes, if only it lasts." His sister Pauline came, too, and ran his household, gave masked dances, and did the usual Italian things. But he kept her short of money, by habit but also because, for the first time in fifteen years, he no longer had millions to spend.

He had 600 men of his Guard with him, and 400 other troops, including Polish lancers. He had a small court and a skeleton administration. Since ancient times Elba had had iron mines and fisheries, and these produced for its government something over a quarter of a million francs a year. The treaty arrangements, signed at his old palace of Fontainebleau, laid it down that the French government was to pay Bonaparte two million francs a year, to which was later added provision for his mother and Pauline. He had his own fortune—not seven million as some said, more like four million—but he wanted to keep that as an "iron reserve." His expenses for the army, administration, and court came to 1.5 million a year. There would have been no problem if the French government had fulfilled its obligations, but it silently refused to send one franc. So almost from the start Bonaparte began to worry about money. He had bitter enemies all over Europe, especially royalists, and he feared they would come to murder him. His army of 1,000 was the least he required to prevent such an attack. He began to sell property and make economies, fearing that the only alternative was reduction in his force. The meanness of the returned Bourbons was not only wrong but (as Talleyrand might have said) a mistake. If Bonaparte had been plentifully pensioned off, the likelihood is that he would have died in Elba, playing with his miniature army. Fear was his strongest motive in seeking a comeback.

Another motive was boredom. Bonaparte was now fat and sometimes sleepy and lazy, but on form he still had more energy than most men. It must be said that, greatly as he liked battles, he also liked doing constructive things. He began by rebuilding his main palace, which had once been a mill, adding a top story. He worked in his garden. He reformed the small administration from top to bottom. He set about improving the iron mines, the roads and bridges and harbors; he introduced agricultural reforms, public instructions, and scientific surveys. This took time, which he had in plenty, but it also cost money, which was short. Parsimonious to himself, Bonaparte hated being less than lavish to others or to the projects on which he set his heart. If the Bourbon regime had paid up, and added a few more millions for "improvements," Bonaparte would have been kept busy and happy, and the vast cost in money and lives of his revanche would have been saved. As it was, the impatient Bonaparte found that all the inexpensive reforms were done within a few months and that further progress in turning his island into a model kingdom would require cash he did not possess. He became bitter, fretful, vengeful. His temper was not improved by the fact that the English upper classes, and many middle-class busybodies, too, had resumed the Grand Tour after years of isolation. They swarmed into Florence, among other places, and it did not require much organization to "take in" Elba and its caged monster. About sixty English tourists alone made the trip and duly gawked. If lucky enough to be introduced, they found the fallen emperor gracious and informative, though he also, as always, asked incessant questions. But Bonaparte, behind his civility, felt exposed and humiliated. He loved to be the cynosure of the brave, when *tête d'armées*—there was no false modesty about him—but he had no relish in the role of fairground wonder.

The third factor in Bonaparte's decision to return was the failure of the restored Bourbons to strike any kind of rapport with the French people. As Talleyrand said: "They have forgotten nothing and learned nothing." To be just to Louis XVIII, he did nothing much wrong. But he was old, fat (Wellington said that pinning the Order of the Garter around his enormous calf was like grasping the waist of a young man), greedy, and obstinate. When he fell down on his first big parade, he refused to be helped to his feet except by the senior officer designated by royal protocol for such a task. Thus he remained supine until the dignitary finally arrived. The contrast between the king and even a defeated emperor was telling. Equally important was the postwar recession, which affected all the belligerents and which brought Britain closer to rebellion than at any time during the previous twenty years. The distress in France, which had only a small industrial sector, was not so great, but it was real and fed the general malaise. Bonaparte was free to receive letters and visitors from France, and both (so he claimed) overwhelmingly urged him to return and save France from its discontents. He certainly exaggerated the desire for yet another overthrow of government. Such quantitative evidence as we possess suggests that, for most Frenchmen, the spell of Bonaparte was broken for good, just as the spell of royalty had been broken in the early 1790s. They left a vacuum of apathy, which could be filled by the vigorous and strongly motivated. The only group that fit this description was the ex-soldiers. Under the emperor they had done well. Now many were without a job and, worse still, without an object in life. But naturally it was to this group Bonaparte listened most. Their entreaties persuaded him that he had no alternative but to become again France's *homme providentiel.* So fear and boredom were joined by destiny, as Bonaparte saw it.

Bonaparte seems to have finally decided to return to France on 15 February 1815, and he then set about preparing his expedition with great speed. If the thing were to be done at all, there was reason for haste. The Bourbons were re-creating the French army, but they were steadily replacing Bonapartist commanders with their own and each month made the force more royalist. Then again, Bonaparte had just got news that the British had made peace with the United States on Christmas Eve 1814, and this meant that the bulk of the British navy's resources, together with Wellington's peninsular veterans, which had recently burned down Washington, would soon be redeployed in the European theater. A more powerful British naval screen would make his expedition impossible. He embarked from Elba on 26 February 1815, aboard a frigate accompanied by six transports, carrying his 600 guardsmen, 100 Polish lancers, a million francs in gold, considerable quantities of ammunition, four guns, and three generals. He had taken elaborate measures to ensure secrecy and steps to mislead by indicating he was heading for Naples (this at first deceived Metternich when he got the news of Bonaparte's disappearance from Elba). The little fleet arrived at Antibes three days later and disembarked its force without opposition.

Bonaparte had achieved total surprise by his plan so far, and he continued to hold the initiative for a time. Indeed all the opening moves of his last campaign showed his military characteristics—surprise, daring, and speed—at their best. From Cannes he took the Alpine route to Grenoble, thus avoiding Marseilles, where the royalist garrison was controlled by Masséna, who had now broken with him for good. Fifteen miles south of Grenoble at Laffrey, he found his route blocked by a regular infantry battalion of the Fifth Regiment. Bonaparte then put on one of his virtuoso performances. He had his military band play the "Marseillaise" and set off alone toward the opposing soldiers. When he was in range of their guns, he got off his horse and walked toward them. Satisfied he was within earshot, he stopped, opened up his greatcoat, and shouted: "It is I, Napoleon. Kill your Emperor if you wish." There was a great silence. Then he told a monstrous lie. "The forty-five wisest men in the Paris government have summoned me from Elba to put France to rights. My return is backed by the three leading powers of Europe." There was another pause; then a shout went up: *"Vive l'empereur!"* The soldiers broke ranks and came to Bonaparte for orders. When the news of this defection reached Paris, it detonated a Jacobin riot, a panic among government ministers, and an upsurge of Bonapartist support in many places. When Bonaparte reached Grenoble, he was greeted as emperor, not indeed by the whole population—far from it—but by a sufficient crowd to speed on the juggernaut. Other regular troops joined him en route to Paris, notably on 14 March at Auxerre, where Marshal Ney, who had been sent with cavalry and orders to arrest Bonaparte, and who had promised "to bring him back in an iron cage," also joined his master. The nerve of the Bourbons finally broke on 19 March, when they left for Ghent, and Bonaparte entered Paris unopposed the next day.

So far, what might have been a desperate venture, ending in squalid failure, had gone spectacularly well, much better than even the optimistic Bonaparte himself had expected. But there had been dramatic changes on the other side, too. Bonaparte had been accustomed to dealing with reluctant coalitions, belatedly formed, slow to move, and divided in their aims. Their armies in particular had always assembled slowly, and their different national commanders had always disputed strategy and often quarreled. But a great change had come over his old opponents. They were now at the head of peoples whose own spirit was up, who had become as nationalist as the French had been for two decades, who identified Bonaparte as the source of the wars that had devastated their countries and cost them fathers, brothers, and sons and who had now revealed himself, once again, as an incorrigible enemy of peace. This was not a sophisticated diplomatic fact that needed explaining. It was an obvious truth, almost a truism now, that stared everyone in the face. So Leipzig, the great Battle of the Nations, had not been enough! More was required, another effort to lay the ghost of the tyrant to rest. So be it! The sovereigns of Europe and their advisers, meeting at Vienna, had already redrawn the map of Europe and reached agreement on many knotty problems. For the first time, they formed what might be called a team. When news of Bonaparte's return reached them—there are conflicting accounts of when and how, and who got it first—the potentates all assembled within hours and their reactions were immediate and unanimous. What had happened was unacceptable and fatal to the tranquillity of Europe. They declared Bonaparte an outlaw, ordered his arrest, and took immediate military steps to make it possible. The speed with which Europe reacted was, for the first time, akin to Bonaparte's own, and it must have come as a disconcerting surprise to him. The Seventh (and final) Coalition came into existence within hours.

There was a second new factor. Wellington, too, was at Vienna, where he had temporarily replaced Castlereagh, the British foreign secretary, as head of the British delegation. His military reputation was now the highest in Europe, for he had beaten all Bonaparte's marshals, if not the master himself. At Vienna he had recently displayed considerable political and diplomatic skills, and won the trust and confidence of the sovereigns and their ministers. They had no doubts about listening to and heeding his military advice, and in effect they put him in charge of their stop-Bonaparte strategy. He was also appointed generalissimo not just of the British forces in Flanders but of such German, Dutch, and Belgian forces as could be quickly gathered in that theater. For Wellington guessed, rightly, that if Bonaparte made a quick forward move, he would head north.

But when? Each of the Allies pledged itself to put at least 150,000 men into the field and keep them there until Bonaparte was destroyed. Bonaparte inherited from the Bourbons a standing army of 150,000, one-third of which he could have brought together by the end of March, making possible a northward thrust starting at the beginning of April. He declined this option for political reasons. It would have stamped him again as the aggressor, and he wanted the Allies to signal their intention to invade France first. In fact, his chances were beyond the help of politics, diplomacy, or propaganda. Only the successful use of force could save him. By throwing away the lightning-attack option, he raised the odds in the Allies' favor. On the other hand, by prodigies of effort from his hastily constituted administration, he had put together a total force of 360,000, of which 180,000 were available for his attack. However, he broke one of his original rules at this point. Instead of committing the whole of his offensive, he limited his own army to about 120,000 and dispersed the rest on the frontiers to resist invasion. He might have added to his force in the coming battle, on which all hinged, another 35,000 men. Who could say what difference this would have made? Bonaparte's third mistake was to deprive himself of the services of Murat, his best and most experienced cavalry commander. When Bonaparte returned, of twenty marshals still active, four stuck to Louis XVIII, three defected to the British-Allied army, one went to the Prussians, and two went into hiding. So Bonaparte had about half of them and a new one, Emmanuel de Grouchy—that is, ten. Or rather, nine, for Murat, having lost his kingdom of Naples, had returned to

France, but Bonaparte decided he could not be forgiven or trusted again. Granted the weakness of his cavalry, this was a self-inflicted wound.

Nothing is more confusing than a detailed and rationalized description of a complex military campaign that probably left most of the participating generals bewildered, and this is one reason why, in this account of Bonaparte, most of his major battles have been given cursory treatment. But Waterloo was essentially a simple affair, of profound historical importance, and so merits a closer look. Bonaparte had to act fast, as with every day that passed, the Allies were gathering more troops and lengthening the numerical odds against him. By the beginning of June 1815, Wellington's Anglo-Dutch-German army, headquartered at Brussels, numbered more than 90,000. Blücher's Prussian army, headquartered at Namur, was about 116,000. They were cantoned over an east-west axis of ninety miles, to a depth of thirty miles. Their geographical concentration point was Charleroi, right in the center of the ninety-mile front.

That was where Bonaparte aimed to strike. He set out from Paris on 11 June, and three days later he had succeeded in drawing together an army distributed along the frontier in an area of 100 by 175 miles into a tight three-part wedge pointed to go for Charleroi. It was fast action and it testified to the quality of Bonaparte's orders, for the "indispensable" chief of staff, Berthier, had refused to join him and he had to make do with Soult, who was more a commanding general than a meticulous staff officer. Up to the beginning of the action, indeed, Bonaparte's writing of orders was fast and skillful and gave no sign of failing powers. Moreover, this rapid concentration took both Wellington and Blücher by surprise, despite all their efforts to keep themselves well informed.

Bonaparte divided his force into two wings (under Ney and Grouchy) and a reserve center, commanded by himself. By moving to Charleroi, his aim, as usual, was to prevent the British and Prussians from joining together in a single defensive mass that would heavily outnumber him. Ney could turn on Wellington, or Grouchy on Blücher—whichever was more exposed—and Bonaparte would be in the center to turn on whichever target gave battle. He thus hoped, as usual, to destroy the two Allied armies separately, with the numerical advantage on his side.

The advance began on 15 June, and when it was held up at the Charleroi bridge over the Sambre, Bonaparte was soon on the spot and took charge of the Young Guard, which promptly stormed the bridge, another sign that he was in good form. With his command post in Charleroi, Bonaparte directed Ney and Grouchy to get to work. The Prussians were heavily handled but withdrew in good order. The British, on the other hand, stubbornly held on to the major crossroads at Quatre Bras, which the French needed to take to force the separation of the Allied armies. Bonaparte's plan, therefore, had not entirely worked, but he still held the strategic initiative and was well placed to carry it out by nightfall, bivouacked in a square of twelve miles each side, right in the center, and in a position to attack either the British or the Prussians.

The two Allied armies were, however, still in contact, and Wellington actually met and discussed plans with Blücher at

Brye, where they could see the French army. The duke was rapidly enforcing his position at Quatre Bras, and fresh troops were reaching his forces all the time. This was of vital importance to him, because he knew he was outnumbered if all Bonaparte's forces were turned upon him. Moreover, he had comparatively few of his peninsular veterans with him, many of his units were of poor quality, and the authorities at home had not allowed him to choose all his own senior officers of staff—they had foisted on him, for instance, Lord Uxbridge to command the cavalry. It would be hard to decide which Wellington distrusted more—the cavalry or their commander. Reinforcements, therefore, were at the forefront of his mind, and if he was to get them and deploy them, the road to his rear had to be kept clear. That is why, in the days leading up to Waterloo, the duke took great pains to appear unconcerned and to conceal his anxieties, which were considerable. Thus he attended the famous ball that the duchess of Richmond gave, not in marble halls as contemporaries such as Byron imagined, but in a Brussels laundry, converted and dressed up for the occasion. Wellington thus prevented a mad panic in Brussels, which would have blocked all his rearward roads with refugees and their gear. Thanks to Wellington's sangfroid, his reinforcements continued to arrive up to and even during the Battle of Waterloo itself and were put straight into action.

It was on 16 June that Bonaparte's plans began to go wrong, though not as yet disastrously so. He ordered Ney to take Quatre Bras, on the left, and decided to use Grouchy's wing and his own center to destroy Blücher, who seemed determined to hold his main position at Ligny. The plan went wrong because the comte d'Erlon, who commanded one army corps, got conflicting instructions from Ney and Bonaparte (this would not have happened if Berthier had been there) and remained in the middle, unengaged. Ney, who might well have taken Quatre Bras with d'Erlon's men, failed, despite heroic personal efforts. Bonaparte's assault on the Prussians at Ligny began early in the afternoon and was pressed with great determination. The Prussians resisted ferociously, and at one point around eight in the evening, Blücher himself led a series of cavalry charges. His horse was shot, fell, and rolled over on him, and he was carried unconscious from the field. But he recovered and eventually resumed the direction of operations. By 9 P.M. it was clear that the Prussians could no longer hold their positions. Indeed, had Bonaparte had d'Erlon's corps, their retreat might have been turned into a rout. As it was, they kept formation and moved back in order, ready to fight again. The losses on both sides were dreadful, more than 20,000 men. At Ligny itself 4,000 men of both sides lay dead in an area of only 400 square yards, and the whole battle had taken place over little more than two square miles. This concentration of the fighting, and so the high number of casualties, was to be a feature of the entire campaign—there had been nearly 10,000 casualties just around the Quatre Bras crossroads.

In view of the Prussians' withdrawal, Wellington early on 17 June decided that remaining in contact with them must override any other consideration, so he withdrew from Quatre Bras and took up a new position on what was to become the field of Waterloo. The failure of either Ney or Bonaparte himself to attack him in strength during this tricky withdrawal was (in the opinion of some) the worst mistake of the entire campaign. Wellington was now in a reasonably strong defensive position, which allowed his men to lie down on the reverse slope to avoid cannon fire, and he was in communication with Blücher, who promised to send between two and four corps to his assistance if he had to take the brunt of the French attack the next day, 18 June. Bonaparte, meanwhile, had sent Grouchy, with 33,000 men and 96 guns, about one-third of the entire army, to follow Blücher and physically prevent him from aiding Wellington. By an extraordinary series of misfortunes, Grouchy ended up to the east of the four corps Blücher was maneuvering toward Waterloo, instead of to the west of them. And for vital hours neither Grouchy nor his master was aware of this fatal misplacement, which made nonsense of Bonaparte's entire strategy of "divide and win."

All the same, at dawn on 18 June, the odds still favored Bonaparte. There had been intermittent thunderstorms over the preceding few days. The ground, chiefly cornfields, was wet. The men on both sides were tired and damp, though mostly in good heart, given the circumstances. Wellington had felt obliged to dispatch a quarter of his force, 17,000 men, to a position eight miles to his right (that is, to the west) to prevent a French encircling movement on that flank. In retrospect it seems a mistake, especially since this force included an entire British division. But it is quite possible that, if the duke had not taken this precaution, Bonaparte might have changed his plan and done exactly what Wellington feared.

What made Bonaparte such a dangerous opponent was his ability to seize upon a gap in his enemy's defenses with extraordinary alertness, and respond to it with an aggressive move at high speed. Detaching this force left Wellington with 30,000 British or King's German Legion troops, who could be depended on, and a mixed bag of 36,000 Dutch, Belgians, and others. Some of these soldiers fought gallantly, but some did not, and Wellington must have begun the day with some apprehension—indeed, we know he did. He had 156 cannon, half British. Bonaparte's army consisted of 74,000 men, all French, and 246 guns. It was drawn up in full view of the British at a distance of 1,300 yards. It was in three lines, the Guard forming the third.

Blücher was marching toward the outnumbered Wellington, but for reasons not his fault, his progress was slow. That gave Bonaparte the chance to attack and destroy Wellington before the Prussians arrived. Indeed, he sent orders to Grouchy to do everything to delay the Prussians still further. Grouchy never carried out these orders, partly because he misread them but mainly because he did not know where he was in relation to all the other forces, French, Prussian, and British. The only explanation for Grouchy's getting himself lost was that he could not read a map. That seems an extraordinary lack in a man given a key command by Bonaparte, the greatest military cartographer of all time. But war is full of such mysteries. Whatever the reason for Grouchy's inactivity, he and his men played no further part in the campaign, and for all the help he gave to his master, he might just as well have been in barracks in Paris.

The failure to halt the Prussians' return to the main battle might not have mattered if Bonaparte had thrust forward with his customary speed. He should have attacked at dawn or at latest 6 A.M. Instead he inspected the field and found it too wet. The start was delayed first till 9 A.M., then till 11:30, to permit the ground to dry. It is, to be sure, not easy for a large mass of cavalry and infantry to advance over sodden ground, on a slightly upward slope. But the loss of five or six hours in ordering the attack, in circumstances where the enemy was being reinforced (for units were still reaching Wellington from his own rear, leaving aside the marching Prussians), was a mistake and went against all Bonaparte's principles of seizing the moment and taking risks for the sake of speed.

The delay suggests that Bonaparte was overconfident about the British. He ignored the advice of his marshals, who had had the experience of facing British infantry, that they were extraordinarily obstinate in holding a defensive position. He also underrated Wellington as a tactical commander in battle. When Soult praised the duke, Bonaparte replied: "That's because he has beaten you." Wellington did not make a comparable mistake in underrating Bonaparte. He thought him worth an extra 40,000 men, which almost doubled the numerical odds against the Allies. But Wellington was a confident man himself. He had fought twenty pitched battles against good French troops and won them all. What surprised him, as he later said, was Bonaparte's declining to maneuver much. He said: "The French came on in the same old way and we drove them off in the same old way." What Wellington meant by this was that Bonaparte began with an artillery barrage from eighty guns, followed by massive cavalry attacks, and then put in his infantry. The barrage failed because Wellington's reverse-slope tactic reduced the casualties to a minimum and kept his men in good heart. The subsequent cavalry assault by a total of eighty French squadrons was a formidable business, but the British had time to form squares and beat them off. Only the most determined cavalry, backed up at close range by infantry, could break well-ordered squares, and this was where Murat's absence was felt. The cavalry lacked persistence and the infantry were a long way behind. So many of the best horsemen in France—including the heavy dragoons of the Old Guard—died in vain. It is true that one of the Dutch-Belgian brigades ran for its life, and two brigades of Uxbridge's cavalry launched an unauthorized attack on the French infantry, achieved an initial success, then got out of control (as was usual) and were badly mauled by the French cavalry. But Wellington expected both mishaps and just carried on, making good the gaps with composure. In short, Bonaparte gained very little during the first three strokes of the battle.

There was now, on his part, a need to destroy Wellington's army as quickly as possible and at whatever cost, for already at 1 P.M. he had got his first glimpse of a Prussian corps on the horizon, marching fast toward the battlefield. So he gave Ney an imperative order to take La Haye Saint, a heavily defended farmhouse right in the center of Wellington's position, without delay. The place was held by the King's German Legion, but they had run out of ammunition and could not immediately be resupplied. Ney attacked them with his customary zeal, and after fierce bayonet fighting they withdrew. But this reverse did not break the Allied line, for Wellington merely reformed and tightened it. By now it was after six in the evening, and the first units of Blücher's army were coming into contact with the French right flank. Their arrival allowed Wellington to weaken his left flank by putting two cavalry brigades behind his battered center, thus ruling out a French breakthrough.

Bonaparte had already recognized the seriousness of his position by sending two battalions of the Old Guard, his weapon of last resource, to block the path of the Prussians at the point of the bayonet. He now, about 7:30, launched his entire line to attack the British position, and threw in the whole of the Old Guard, less five battalions. The attack was vigorous but so was the defense, and the terrible cry went up in the French army: *"La Garde recule!"* (the Guard is falling back). That dismal sound had never been heard before in a battle with Bonaparte in command. Indeed, the retreat of the Old Guard, orderly but nonetheless definitive, gave Wellington the opportunity to wave his hat and call out: "Stand up, Guards, and move forward." After a desperate day on the defensive, the British and their allies now themselves attacked, closely followed by their guns, which pounded into the retreating French formations. At the same time, the Prussians, in growing numbers, were rolling up the right of the French position. Two battalions of the French Old Guard, from the first regiment of grenadiers, refused to move and had to be blown to pieces by cannon at point-blank range. But the rest of the army became a hunted rabble, scattering in all directions.

By 9 P.M. it was all over, and Wellington and Blücher met fifteen minutes later at another battered farmhouse, La Belle Alliance. Blücher said to the duke: *"Mon dieu, quelle affaire!"* It was almost the only French he knew, but it summed up well a dreadful day. The fighting had taken place almost entirely in a narrow area of less than three square miles, and this sodden field was now covered with dead and dying men and horses. There had been spectacular heroism on all sides. Ney had fought like a lion, surviving as half a dozen horses were killed under him, and finally leading his men directly at the English guards on foot. His last observed act on the battlefield was to vent his frustration on his sword, which he struck and broke against the barrel of an abandoned cannon. He wanted to die in action because he knew that his life would be exacted for his blatant desertion of his king, as indeed it was.

When Bonaparte had broken the news to his mother that he was leaving Elba to fight again, she had said to him: "Good. Better to die with your sword in hand than waste the rest of your life in exile." But Bonaparte took no opportunity to involve himself in the mêlée. He was probably afraid not of death but of capture. Indeed, if he had fallen into the hands of the Prussians, Blücher would probably have shot him. Wellington said he never saw Bonaparte during the smoky inferno of the battle, though Soult, whom he had seen before, he recognized without difficulty, as he issued orders. As darkness finally fell on the long, horrifying day, Bonaparte took to his coach, protected by a screen of cavalry. But the mud soon forced him to get onto a horse and ride as hard as he could to safety. He made no comment on the scale of the

French losses, which were 40,000 on the field of Waterloo alone. Blücher had lost 7,000 men during the final hours of the day. Wellington had lost 15,000, including some of his best generals and officers and many personal friends. He was untouched, like Bonaparte himself, but Uxbridge had lost a leg to cannon shot in the closing minutes of the battle, while he and Wellington were in conversation. The duke was visibly shaken by the carnage and kept repeating to Thomas Creevey, a Whig MP: "It was a close-run thing, a damn close-run thing. I do not think it would have done if I had not been there." The harrowing experience of Waterloo gave rise to one of his most earnest remarks: "There is nothing in life worse than a battle won, except a battle lost." His final verdict on Bonaparte's conduct was that he would have been infinitely wiser to have fought a defensive campaign, which would have raised great, possibly insuperable, problems for the Allies. "But then he was always too impatient for that."

Waterloo was one of the decisive battles of history and brought to an end the entire Revolutionary and Napoleonic period. On 20 June, Bonaparte handed over command of what was left of the army to Soult. The French armed forces were by no means finished—about 150,000 men were operating in various formations and 175,000 conscripts were in training—but the French elites had had enough. Fouché, who wanted a powerful role for himself under the Bourbons, persuaded the so-called representative institutions, the Chamber of Deputies and the Senate, to call for Bonaparte's abdication, and he obliged on 21 June. He was not sure what he ought or wanted to do next. He had some vague project for going to

America, probably the United States. Latin America was now in full revolt against Spanish rule, and Bonaparte was not the only one to see a future for himself there: Byron was considering fitting out a force to join in the struggle. Frustrated in Europe, Bonaparte was later to talk of a scheme to create an enormous nation in the Americas of 100 million people. But he had first to get there. He headed for the port of Rochefort, hoping to take ship for New York or Boston. But when he arrived, on 3 July, he found the British navy had forestalled him. After five more days of hesitation, he decided that his best course was to give himself up to the British, whom he described, in an appeal for refuge to the prince regent, as "the most powerful, the most unwavering and the most generous of [my] foes." He climbed aboard a frigate that took him to the Île d'Aix, where he was transferred to HMS *Bellerophon,* a captured French battleship now known in the British fleet as the "Billy Ruffian." His flattery got him nowhere. He was taken to Plymouth, where he remained for three weeks, an object of great interest to the local population, who were taken out by the boatload to see him. Bonaparte obliged by parading at the entry port, in full uniform, at the same time every day. But the grim truth became daily more obvious to him. He was not to be given his freedom, and the delay was occasioned only by the need for consultation among the Allies about where he was to be sent and held. The dread words "Saint Helena," first uttered the previous year as an alternative to Elba, now took irrevocable shape. Despite an attempt by his Whig friends to have a writ of habeas corpus served on the warship's commander, Bonaparte remained under custody and was transferred to HMS *Northumberland;* the ship sailed for the prison-island just before the end of the month, arriving there on 17 October 1815. Bonaparte was forty-five. Had these events occurred at the beginning of the present century, there can be little doubt that Bonaparte would have been obliged to face a war crimes tribunal, with an inevitable verdict of "guilty" and a sentence of death or life imprisonment. The evidence then produced would have determined, forever, in the minds of reasonable people, the degree of guilt he bore for events that had cost four or five million lives and immense loss of property. In his day, however, no precedents for such a procedure and no machinery existed; he went to his captivity untried, by an act of state on the part of the British government, with, to be sure, the agreement of all the other European governments and the tacit approval of the French. The consequence was another example of Popper's law of unintended effect—the birth of the Napoleonic legend.

CHAPTER SEVEN

The Long Good-bye

THE DECISION to confine Bonaparte on Saint Helena was taken at the Vienna Congress, confirmed at the Conference of Aix-la-Chapelle, and made lawful in the English courts by an act of Parliament that designated him as a prisoner of war under the name of General Bonaparte. Saint Helena was a volcanic island, twenty-eight miles in circumference, in the South Atlantic, used as a watering station on the route to India. It had a typical oceanic climate, with frequent showers and occasional mist, and those living there tended to suffer from amoebic dysentery. Otherwise it was reasonably healthy. As the island was a frequent port of call for naval and mercantile ships on a major trade route, it combined accessibility with great distance from any sympathizers likely to attempt a rescue, and in fact during the six years Bonaparte lived on the island no serious effort was made to organize his escape. Distance was reinforced by a squadron of frigates kept on permanent station around the island, an inshore patrol of brigs, and a garrison of 2,250 men. The number of cannon emplaced to resist assault was raised to 500. The cost to the British taxpayer was nearly half a million gold napoleons a year.

Bonaparte was permitted to take with him a group of courtiers and a dozen servants—his Mamluk bodyguard, a butler, a cook, three valets, three footmen, an accountant, a pantryman, and a lamp cleaner. The servants gave no trouble. Indeed, Louis Marchand, the young head body servant, refuted the axiom that no great man is a hero to his valet: he worshiped the fallen emperor. The courtiers were a different matter. One, the marquis Charles de Montholon, was probably chosen because he had a pretty wife, Albine, who (it is generally supposed) became Bonaparte's last mistress, but she also took one of the English officers as a lover and departed under a cloud. Another, General Gaspar Gourgaud, was an excitable man, perhaps a homosexual (he sometimes referred to Bonaparte as "she"), who was jealous of Montholon and his wife and challenged the marquis to a duel. He, too, left under a cloud. There was also a civilian lawyer, Count Joseph de Las Cases, and his son Emmanuel. But Las Cases was deported for breaking the rules of the imprisonment, by smuggling out letters. The senior member of the entourage was General Count Henri Bertrand, who had been Bonaparte's palace marshal and was almost his age. Unfortunately his wife, Fanny, was a royalist, who had tried to drown herself when told she must accompany her husband into exile, and Bonaparte compounded her antipathy, after the departure of Albine, by making a pass at her, which was violently rebuffed. Various other people joined the court during the exile. There were priests, sent by Madame Mère and Bonaparte's uncle Cardinal Fesch, who made little impact on the highly secular prisoner, and doctors, of whom Dr. Barry O'Meara, a surgeon from the *Bellerophon,* was the most significant. There were between twelve and sixteen courtiers in all.

History shows, not least in our own times, that all courts, especially when they are small and in exile, are seething circles of jealousy and intrigue, and Bonaparte's was a characteristic example of this unlovable phenomenon. At times the hatred was almost palpable and accusations of betrayal flew around. At one stage Bonaparte expressed the view that he should have taken with him only servants, and one cannot help agreeing with him. The significance of the courtiers was that they took down Bonaparte's own rambling reminiscences, and six of them, plus one of the valets, also produced memoirs of their own, which became the basis of the huge Napoleon literature industry that began to develop from 1816 onward and continues relentlessly to this day. These memoirs, like everything else concerning Bonaparte's life, disagree markedly, often on plain matters of fact, and reflect the tensions and antipathies of the exile, which was as dramatic in its own way as any other period of his life.

The chief source of the drama, other than the ex-emperor himself, was the dull, obstinate, dutiful, meticulous, well-meaning, honest, nervous, and overscrupulous Hudson Lowe, who had been appointed governor and jailer in chief of the prisoner. No one of any pull or importance in England wanted the job, and Lowe, who was not a gentleman by birth, was glad to get it. It meant affluence to him—£12,000 a year plus perks—and included a Knight Commander of the Order of the Bath (he had already been knighted) and the local rank of lieutenant general. Lowe's father had been a regimental surgeon. Lowe was born into the army *en poste*, joined it at the age of twelve, and served it all his life, throughout the empire and the European theater. Bonaparte sneered at him for never having heard a shot fired in anger, but this was totally untrue. Lowe was present at thirty-one battles (against Bonaparte's fifty), being witness both to Bonaparte's Egyptian campaign and to his defeat at Leipzig. Lowe fought in Italy, Germany, Greece, Spain, and France itself, being presented with a testimonial from the citizens of Marseilles for saving them from pillage. He spoke a number of languages and became a specialist, first, in raising and training local corps—such as the Corsican Rangers, the Malta Regiment, the Neapolitan irregulars, and the Russo-German Legion, all financed by the British government—and second, in liaising with Allied armies, especially the Prussians; thus he acted as aide-de-camp to Blücher in thirteen battles. He was a versatile and experienced man, officially cited as "never having been absent from his duty a single day since the beginning of the war in 1793." The duke of Wellington, who had had him as quartermaster general, thought him far from clever but a conscientious and scrupulously honest officer, who had been the victim of a scandalous campaign of abuse.

Whence came this abuse? In England it was orchestrated by the Holland House circle of Whigs, who had always sympathized with Bonaparte as an opponent of absolute monarchy by divine right, and were anxious to effect his release or escape. Having failed to serve a habeas corpus writ, Lord and Lady Holland, immediately after Lowe's appointment was announced, invited him repeatedly to Holland House and used all their considerable charm and flattery to bring him around to their viewpoint and persuade him to impose the lightest of regimes on his famous prisoner. Lowe was bewildered at first, thus to be brought into the most exclusive society in Europe, but soon realized what the Hollands were up to. He made it clear he intended to follow closely the instructions of Earl Bathurst, the colonial secretary, endorsed by the cabinet and Parliament, that Bonaparte was to be afforded every consideration compatible with security. At that point the Hollands dropped him and thereafter became his dedicated enemies.

On the island itself, the campaign was deliberately conducted by the court. Bonaparte himself began by trying to charm Lowe but quickly realized he was incorruptible. Thereafter Lowe was characterized as Satan: mean, suspicious, mendacious, bribing his servants, an expert poisoner, and a man capable of the basest cruelty, who had led a gang of murderous Corsican brigands. It is often implied that Lowe and Bonaparte were in daily dispute about trifles, the small-minded Lowe contrasted with the magnanimous Bonaparte. In fact they met only six times, and the last two conversations consisted entirely of abuse on Bonaparte's side and silence on Lowe's.

Bonaparte had always, as we have noted, been good at propaganda, from Italy and Egypt onward, and now, encouraged and assisted by Holland House, he began the most prolonged and successful propaganda campaign of his life. It was summed up by Basil Jackson, a young British officer on guard duty around Bonaparte:

The policy—heartily and assiduously carried out by Napoleon's adherents, who liked banishment as little as the great man himself—was to pour into England pamphlets and letters complaining of unnecessary restrictions, insults from the governor, scarcity of provisions, miserable accommodation, insalubrity of climate, and a host of other grievances, but chiefly levelled at the governor, as the head and front of all that was amiss.

Later, after Bonaparte was dead, de Montholon admitted to Jackson: *"C'était nôtre politique, et que voulez-vous?"* ("It was our policy—but what did you expect?")

The truth is, Lowe was a humane man, as numerous episodes in his life show. In 1808 he had appealed personally to Bonaparte's close colleague Berthier against the mass executions carried out by the French army of Naples against Calabrian patriots. He was highly popular with the civilian populations in the various administrative posts he held in Italy and the Ionian Islands, being presented with testimonials and swords of honor in gratitude. He was popular, too, in Saint Helena, among all classes, even the landowners, despite the fact that, by his own act of prerogative, he ended slavery there in 1817, sixteen years before it was abolished in the empire as a whole. The islanders were sad to see him go, soon after Bonaparte's death (he was succeeded by the lugubrious Brigadier John Pine Coffin).

There is no evidence that Lowe treated Bonaparte meanly or cruelly. On the contrary, it was Lowe who raised the sum allocated to Bonaparte's household from £8,000 a year to

£12,000, equal to his own as governor. The later reduction to the original sum was a diktat from the Colonial Office, which left Lowe with no choice. He must have smiled grimly to himself at Bonaparte's blaming the resulting economies entirely on Government House, accompanied by ostentatious propaganda devices, such as the public sale of his silver and the breaking up of furniture for firewood. In fact Bonaparte did not go short of anything. Longwood, in which he was eventually established, was probably the best house on the island, with more than forty rooms. It had a fine library, and Lowe also offered access to his own large collection of books (it was declined). The restrictions on Bonaparte's riding and walking—that he be accompanied at all times by a British officer, when outside the grounds of Longwood—were minimal. The restrictions on his correspondence were more irksome, but entirely justified, in view of what we now know.

Lowe was in an impossible position. Bonaparte was not held as a close prisoner, or even under house arrest. He had a court and staff and a legion of supporters in the outside world, even in England—people in high positions and of great means. Lowe had to ensure, on peril of his life, that he prevented from escaping the most dangerous man Europe had ever suffered from, who was responsible for the deaths of millions and wars that had kept the entire Continent in an uproar for a decade and a half. Bonaparte's word was worthless. He had broken every treaty he had ever signed, most notably the agreement that set him up in some style in Elba. This last perjury had cost the lives of nearly 100,000 brave men and huge destruction of property. If Bonaparte was at large again, what further pain and misery might he not inflict on innocent people by the insensate pursuit of his ambition? These considerations made Lowe strict, and Europe had reason to be grateful that he was.

Bonaparte's metier was army command. His purpose in life—one must not, perhaps, say his delight—was battle. Naturally, on Saint Helena he was unhappy. He needed women on call. He needed excitement. He needed, above all, events. But there were no events on Saint Helena. He dug in the garden. He dictated. He tried to learn to speak and write English, without success, as a scrap in his handwriting, dated 7 March 1816, testifies: "Count Lascasses. Since sixt wek, y lern the english and y do not any progres. Sixt wek do fourty and two day. If might have learn fivty word, for day, I could knowm it two thousands and two hundred." He discoursed endlessly. He held soirées, even a dance occasionally. He had periods of acute depression or illness, chiefly digestive, in which he appeared to none but his servants. He visited and received visitors. He played whist with the English officers. He stood, gazing out to sea, as he had often stood on the battlefield, a small, squat, rounded figure, in an old gray greatcoat, his hat planted firmly on his massive brow.

Thus he was seen and described. On 8 March 1817 the *Prince Regent* put into the island. Aboard were the five-year-old William Makepeace Thackeray, returning from India for school in England, and his black servant, Lawrence Barlow. Barlow, the future novelist recorded later, "took me a long walk over rocks and hills until we reached a garden, where we saw a man walking. 'That is he,' said the black man, 'that is

Bonaparte! He eats three sheep every day and as many little children as he can lay his hands on!'" Impressions of those who actually met Bonaparte varied. The sailor who took him out to Saint Helena, George Cockburn, took a liking to him but deplored his unfriendly habit of leaving the table as soon as he had bolted his food. Betsy Briars, the fourteen-year-old daughter of the East India Company agent on the island, made a real friend of the ex-emperor, though she accused him of cheating at cards (she was not the only one to make the charge). He was sad when she returned to England in 1818, and she remembered him with love and kisses, and talked to Napoleon III about his famous relative, being rewarded with the gift of a vineyard in Algeria. Some visitors had the good fortune to be received by the great man and reported him to be affable, asking numerous questions as was his wont, but not always listening to the answers. From 1819 onward his personal appearances became less frequent and from the middle of 1820 he was a sick man who kept mostly to his house.

As Bonaparte's death became part of his mythology, it is necessary to dwell on it in a little detail. He was attended, at one time or another, by at least six doctors during his last illness, which began on 17 March 1821 and ended with his death on 5 May. They disagreed about the treatment, as did his court. His symptoms included a swollen stomach, slow pulse, rising and falling temperature, vomiting and coughing, abundant sweating and nausea, delirium, shivering, hiccups, and, eventually, loss of memory and delusions. He was dosed with mercury and calomel but, in his more authoritative moments, he refused to take medicine or even see his doctors. He also declined to be administered to by the two priests his family had sent out, saying he had no religion; but they secretly gave him the last rites all the same. When clearheaded, he revised his will. Two of the changes are significant. First, he left 10,000 francs to André Cantillon, the old soldier who in Paris on 11 February 1818 had tried to shoot Wellington but had been released for lack of witnesses. Second, the fifth paragraph read: "My death is not natural. I have been assassinated by the English oligarchy and their hired murderer (Lowe). The English people will not be long in avenging me."

Whether Bonaparte actually believed he was poisoned is doubtful, though he made the accusation repeatedly, long before he stated it in writing in his will. But then he made many wild accusations in Saint Helena. He abused Madame Bertrand, for instance, as "a whore, who should have walked the streets as an ordinary prostitute: she has slept with all the English officers of the garrison." In his Italian-Corsican way, he often thought of the risk of poison and had accused all kinds of enemies of trying it against him, throughout his career. He was not an easy man to poison, it seems. The only occasion when poison was actually administered to him, by himself in a suicide dose taken in March 1814, the dose—"strong enough to kill two of his troopers," according to the account—had no effect at all. This may have been due to the incompetence or deviousness of his court physician, Jean Corvisart. Or perhaps the whole story is an invention. Bonaparte was certainly not a suicidal type, and he made no effort to kill himself in July 1815, when he had a much stronger motive. Many Bonapartist historians have mooted the theory of arsenical poisoning, though they have disagreed about whether it was given in small or large doses, and the direct scientific evidence is inconclusive. It is inconceivable that Lowe could or would have administered it on the instructions of the cabinet. Indeed, Bonaparte himself, from time to time, thought a more likely killer would have been the comte d'Artois, the future Charles X, or "white" terrorists, or the Russians or Prussians.

Bonaparte's whole medical history, needless to say, has been examined in great detail by doctors with historical tastes. Considering the life he led and the risks he took, he was a fortunate man in health. He was probably present at more military engagements, and within cannon and rifle shot, than any other man of his time, including Ney and Wellington, though both ran him close. He had at least nineteen horses killed under him in battle (and he spurred to death many more). At Toulon he was wounded in the face and had a bayonet thrust into the inner side of his left thigh, a wound (he said) that bothered him always. His other battle wounds, though numerous, were all superficial. He joked that one of the worst was inflicted by Josephine's jealous lapdog during the "battle" of their wedding night. There are stories that he contracted gonorrhea (from Josephine) and syphilis, but no direct evidence of either exists.

Bonaparte obviously feared he would go the same way as his father, who had died of stomach cancer. He often complained about abdominal pains throughout his life. He ate moderately and drank his wine watered. On the other hand, he gobbled his meals in ten minutes if he could. He took vigorous exercise on horseback throughout all his active life. Nonetheless, from about the age of thirty he began to put on weight, and his body began to acquire the pale-pink fatty appearance that became notable in his last phase and that led people to compare him to a china pig. He had blackouts when making love on several occasions (his women complained that he copulated ardently but quickly and without regard to them). There was intermittent trouble with his chest, though no sign of tuberculosis, then the second biggest killer of youngish men. From about 1810 he had trouble passing water. This caused him much distress during the Russian campaign and again during the Hundred Days. From the very start of his Saint Helena sojourn he complained of constipation, stomachaches, and vomiting, but said his chief hardship was passing water. Indeed, he was seen several times leaning against a wall or a tree, trying to urinate, and was heard to groan: "This is my weak spot—this will kill me in the end."

Bonaparte was officially pronounced dead by the Florentine doctor Francesco Antommarchi, who proceeded to carry out a postmortem examination, watched by five English surgeons, Mitchell, Livingstone, Arnott, Burton, and Shortt, who signed the report, and a sixth, Henry, who drew it up but was too junior to sign it. Their conclusion was that Bonaparte had died of a cancerous ulcer or carcinoma in his stomach, and they reached this verdict without knowing that the dead man's father had suffered the same fate. Antommarchi refused to sign this report, producing one of his own that indicated that an enlarged liver, presumably caused by hepatitis, was the cause. Both reports describe the condition of the body. The teeth were healthy but stained black by the chewing of licorice. The left kidney was one-third larger than the right. The urinary bladder was small and it contained gravel; the mucosa was thickened with numerous red patches. Had the urethra been sectioned (or so runs one theory) it would probably have demonstrated a small circular scar, too tight to allow the passing of even small stones. That would have been the key to the slow decline in health and performance that started when Bonaparte was in his late thirties. The body was what doctors call "feminized"—that is, covered by a deep layer of fat, with scarcely any hair and well-developed breasts and mons veneris. The shoulders were narrow, hips broad, and genitals small. We can all make up our own minds about these findings, their significance and reliability.

The news of Bonaparte's death reached London on 3 July. George IV was told: "It is my duty to inform your Majesty that your greatest enemy is dead." He replied: *"Is she, by God!"* (he thought the ailing Queen Caroline was meant). Wellington got the news the next day in Paris, at a party attended by Talleyrand. Someone, on hearing the news, exclaimed: *"Quelle événement!"* Talleyrand dryly replied: *"Non, ce n'est pas un événement, c'est une nouvelle."* (Not an event, just a news item.) Wellington's friend Mrs. Arbuthnot recorded in her diary of 4 July: "The Duke of Wellington called on me and said, 'Now I think I may say I am the most successful Gen[eral] alive.'"

The death of Napoleon Bonaparte did not long remain a news item. His last words had been—so it was said—*"tête d'armée,"* and he was buried as a soldier, in his favorite green uniform of the Guards cavalry, and the famous gray overcoat he had worn at Marengo. The site was the Rupert Valley, a beautiful place, and the grave was marked by a stone that bore only the words CI-GIT ("here lies"), because the French and the English could not agree on the inscription. It might have been better for the world, including France, if this simple *enterrement* had been left undisturbed. For if Bonaparte had died as a stricken and defeated man, Napoleon soon began to rise as an immortal myth, a victorious soldier, and a model ruler. The returned Bourbons had never been popular, and in 1830 they were sent packing by the Paris mob. And even the Bourbons had been unable to prevent the emergence of a Napoleon industry. It began effectively with the publication of Las Cases's *Memorial de Saint-Hélène* (1822–23), an immensely popular account of the exile, full of falsehoods and exaggerations but successfully designed to evoke sympathy for a stricken giant in the chains of an alien pygmy. Other memoirs, following the same "policy," by Gourgaud, Montholon, and Bertrand, followed. The poets, led by Pierre-Jean de Béranger, soon took a hand: *Souvenirs du peuple,* nostalgic for former glories, appeared in 1828. And Victor Hugo, who had welcomed the Bourbons back, switched sides and began to write impassioned poems in Napoleon's honor, beginning with *Ode de la Colonne,* which dates from 1827. Soon, virtually all the considerable forces of French literature were hard at work, and the powerful Paris printing industry produced cheaply a colored picture history of Napoleon's life and achievements that sold hundreds of thousands of copies, was lovingly treasured by the poor, and was the first introduction to history for generations of French children.

This was the buildup to official rehabilitation—indeed, glorification. Louis-Philippe, succeeding the Bourbons in 1830, significantly called himself "king of the French," in imitation of Napoleonic populism. In 1833 he put back Napoleon's statue on top of the column in the Place Vendôme in Paris. In 1830, too, the Whigs at last got power in England, ousting the Wellington government. Bonaparte, in his will, had asked to be buried "on the banks of the Seine." Lord Holland, now a minister, repeatedly urged that the wish be respected; at last in 1840 the British government agreed, and the body was dug up. Louis-Philippe sent his son François in a warship to collect the remains of the man now universally known in France as "the emperor." A magnificent funeral was held in Paris in December 1840, before the body was conveyed to the historic military *hôpital* of the Invalides, created by Louis XIV and turned by Bonaparte himself into a military pantheon. There, over the next twenty years, the most sumptuous tomb-memorial since antiquity was prepared, under the dome, for the glorification of "the greatest soldier who ever lived." The light streams down theatrically onto the catafalque in one of the greatest visual frissons of tourist Paris—vulgar certainly, but spectacular and unforgettable.

The legend achieved its first major impact on history in December 1851, when Bonaparte's nephew Louis-Napoleon exploited it to stage a coup d'état in the manner of his uncle and made himself "emperor of the French" the following year. The Napoleon industry thereafter received official backing and financial support.

Newspapers with titles like *Le Petit Caporal* and *Le Redingote gris* flourished. By order of Napoleon III, twenty-eight enormous volumes of Bonaparte's correspondence, plus three volumes of his Saint Helena writings and a final volume of his will and Orders of the Day, were published in 1858-70, many distinguished French writers assisting in this vast undertaking. Some demurred. Lamartine, originally in favor that justice be done to Bonaparte, protested against what he called "this Napoleonic religion, this cult of force which is being infused into the spirit of the nation instead of the true religion of liberty." But most bowed the knee to the legend of the man who now epitomized French greatness—a greatness that was fast fading. The collapse of the second Napoleonic Empire in the catastrophe of Sedan—recalling Marx's epigram "History first enacts itself as tragedy, then repeats itself as farce," which applies to the fall of both Napoleons as well as their rise—merely intensified the nostalgic urge to remember the years when the Napoleonic nation bestrode the world. So the republic of Clemençeau, the Vichy dictatorship of Pétain, the Fourth Republic of existentialist chaos, and the Fifth Republic of de Gaulle all genuflected at the tomb and venerated its occupant.

Perhaps more seriously, in the long run, the Napoleonic cult spread and produced a monstrous progeny. The British, who might have been expected to restore sense, balance, and truth amid the uproar, in fact did the opposite. The cult in England began with O'Meara's Saint Helena memoir of 1822, which eulogized Bonaparte and vilified Lowe. The infuriated ex-governor spent the rest of his life and his savings in vain attempts to nail O'Meara's lies. No one read Hazlitt's hagiography, but many thousands bought Walter Scott's *Life of Napoleon*, which, though critical, also uses the Stricken Giant theme to promote sympathy for fallen greatness. Others went further. Emerson, the most popular and influential American writer of the mid-nineteenth century, praised Bonaparte as "the agent or attorney of the middle classes" and cited him as the archetype of the admirable "self-made man" (a phrase then coming into vogue). Samuel Smiles, the evangelist of self-help, hailed him as the supreme exemplar; Belloc and Chesterton, Hardy and Shaw hailed the Napoleon of legend variously as "the savior of Europe," the emperor of the people, and the true Superman.

In retrospect, the most significant of the British Napoleonists was Thomas Carlyle, who brought Bonaparte center stage in his celebrated lectures of 1841, *Heroes and Hero Worship*. Like most of the other writers, Carlyle conceded that Bonaparte had had a fatal moral flaw, which had undone him; but he was, nonetheless, the "true Democrat," "our last Great Man." Admiration for Bonaparte led him to undertake his immense biography of Frederick II, which transfixed Germany with excitement and which Goebbels read to Hitler for mutual solace during their last days in the Berlin bunker of 1945. Thanks to the verse of Heine, the most popular of all German lyric poets, the myth of Napoleon, the strong ruler, "the Man on Horseback," had already found a home in Germany, where the all-powerful state conceived by his old admirer Hegel became the taproot for both Marxist and Nazi totalitarianism. Mussolini, a mountebank dictator like Napoleon III, had a Napoleonic streak, down to his cult of ancient Rome and his endless colonnades. Albert Speer, Hitler's architect and *apprenti sorcier,* was a Bonapartist, too, and his relationship to his master had strange parallels with Denon's to the emperor. No dictator of the tragic twentieth century—from Lenin, Stalin, and Mao Zedong to pygmy tyrants like Kim Il Sung, Castro, Perón, Mengistu, Saddam Hussein, Ceauşescu, and Gadhafi—was without distinctive echoes of the Napoleonic prototype. It is curious indeed that Bonaparte, in his lifetime, quite failed to destroy legitimist Europe. In the end, he provoked the Congress of Vienna, which refounded legitimism so firmly that it lasted another century until, in the First World War, it destroyed itself. Instead, the great evils of Bonapartism—the deification of force and war, the all-powerful centralized state, the use of cultural propaganda to apotheosize the autocrat, the marshaling of entire peoples in the pursuit of personal and ideological power—came to hateful maturity only in the twentieth century, which will go down in history as the Age of Infamy. It is well to remember the truth about the man whose example gave rise to it all, to strip away the myth and reveal the reality. We have to learn again the central lesson of history: that all forms of greatness, military and administrative, nation and empire building, are as nothing—indeed are perilous in the extreme—without a humble and a contrite heart.

Further Reading

THE THIRTY-TWO VOLUMES of Napoleon's correspondence, in French, were reprinted in Paris in 1974. Two volumes were published in English in 1946, his correspondence with his brother Joseph in English in two volumes in 1855, and further official military correspondence in three volumes in English in 1913. What he wrote and said about himself is collected in various works such as J. M. Thompson (ed.), *Napoleon Self-Revealed* (1934), and Christopher Herrold (ed.), *The Mind of Napoleon* (1955). There are a number of Napoleonic dictionaries, mainly in French, such as André Palluel (ed.), *Dictionnaire de l'Empéreur* (1969). There are two excellent short lives of Napoleon in English: H. A. L. Fisher, *Napoleon* (1913), and Herbert Butterfield, *Napoleon* (1945). Among the pro-Napoleon biographies in English are J. Holland Rose, *A Life of Napoleon* (reissued in 1935), and Frank McLynn, *Napoleon: A Biography* (1998). J. M. Thompson, *Napoleon Bonaparte: His Rise and Fall* (reissued 1969), is more critical. Another critical work is Pierre Lanfrey, *The History of Napoleon I,* originally in French, in four volumes, in 1867–75, reprinted in English in 1973. French hagiographies of Napoleon are innumerable. For critical views by his contemporaries, see Chateaubriand, *Mémoires d'outre-tombe,* available in the Pléiade series, and Germaine de Staël, *Dix années d'exile* (1821). There is a brilliant summation of the case against Napoleon by the great French

189

historian Hippolyte Taine in *The Origins of Contemporary France* (English edition, 1974). Wellington's views on Napoleon are to be found in Lord Stanhope, *Conversations with Wellington,* available in the Oxford Classics; and for a comparison of the two men see Andrew Roberts's excellent *Napoleon and Wellington* (2001). For the military campaigns, the best course is to consult D. D. Horward (ed.), *Napoleonic Military History: A Bibliography* (1986). An excellent recent book on the Waterloo campaign is Gregor Dallas, *1815: The Roads to Waterloo* (1996). I also recommend the various books by Alistair Horne on the subject, beginning with his admirable *Napoleon: Master of Europe 1805–7* (1979). For Napoleon's marriages, see Evangeline Bruce, *Napoleon and Josephine* (1996), and Alan Palmer, *Napoleon and Marie-Louise* (2000). For the medical aspects, see J. Henry Dibble, *Napoleon's Surgeon* (1970); James O. Robinson, "The Failing Health of Napoleon," *Journal of the Royal Society of Medicine,* August 1979; and Frank Giles, *Napoleon Bonaparte: England's Prisoner* (2001). For the Napoleon cult, see Jean Lucas-Dubreton, *Le Culte de Napoléon* (1960), and E. Tangye Lean, *The Napoleonists* (1970).

FOR THE BEST IN PAPERBACKS, LOOK FOR THE

In every corner of the world, on every subject under the sun, Penguin represents quality and variety—the very best in publishing today.

For complete information about books available from Penguin—including Penguin Classics, Penguin Compass, and Puffins—and how to order them, write to us at the appropriate address below. Please note that for copyright reasons the selection of books varies from country to country.

In the United States: Please write to *Penguin Group (USA), P.O. Box 12289 Dept. B, Newark, New Jersey 07101-5289* or call 1-800-788-6262.

In the United Kingdom: Please write to *Dept. EP, Penguin Books Ltd, Bath Road, Harmondsworth, West Drayton, Middlesex UB7 0DA.*

In Canada: Please write to *Penguin Books Canada Ltd, 90 Eglinton Avenue East, Suite 700, Toronto, Ontario M4P 2Y3.*

In Australia: Please write to *Penguin Books Australia Ltd, P.O. Box 257, Ringwood, Victoria 3134.*

In New Zealand: Please write to *Penguin Books (NZ) Ltd, Private Bag 102902, North Shore Mail Centre, Auckland 10.*

In India: Please write to *Penguin Books India Pvt Ltd, 11 Panchsheel Shopping Centre, Panchsheel Park, New Delhi 110 017.*

In the Netherlands: Please write to *Penguin Books Netherlands bv, Postbus 3507, NL-1001 AH Amsterdam.*

In Germany: Please write to *Penguin Books Deutschland GmbH, Metzlerstrasse 26, 60594 Frankfurt am Main.*

In Spain: Please write to *Penguin Books S. A., Bravo Murillo 19, 1° B, 28015 Madrid.*

In Italy: Please write to *Penguin Italia s.r.l., Via Benedetto Croce 2, 20094 Corsico, Milano.*

In France: Please write to *Penguin France, Le Carré Wilson, 62 rue Benjamin Baillaud, 31500 Toulouse.*

In Japan: Please write to *Penguin Books Japan Ltd, Kaneko Building, 2-3-25 Koraku, Bunkyo-Ku, Tokyo 112.*

In South Africa: Please write to *Penguin Books South Africa (Pty) Ltd, Private Bag X14, Parkview, 2122 Johannesburg.*